THE HOLY SPIRIT OF LIFE

Essays Written for John Ashcroft's Secret Self

THE HOLY SPIRIT OF LIFE

Essays Written for John Ashcroft's Secret Self

JOE WENDEROTH

VERSE PRESS / AMHERST, MA

Published by Verse Press

Verse Press titles are distributed to the trade by Consortium Book Sales
and Distribution, 1045 Westgate Drive, St. Paul, Minnesota 55114.

Library of Congress Cataloging-in-Publication Data:

Wenderoth, Joe.
 The holy spirit of life : essays written for John Ashcroft's secret
self / Joe Wenderoth.—1st ed.
    p. cm.
 ISBN-13: 978-0-9746353-7-8 (pbk. : alk. paper)
 ISBN-10: 0-9746353-7-5 (pbk. : alk. paper)
 I. Title.
 PS3573.E515H65 2005
 814'.54—dc22
                    2005007248

Cover Photograph: Dr. Tim Boehme. Used by permission.
Design and composition by J. Johnson.
Text set in Sabon. Display set in Knockout.

Printed in the United States of America

9 8 7 6 5 4 3 2 1

First Edition

for Educated Bowlers

and for fans of Educated Bowlers

The preaching of chastity is a public incitement to anti-nature. Every expression of contempt for the sexual life, every befouling of it through the concept of "impurity," is *the* crime against life—is the intrinsic sin against the holy spirit of life.

—Nietzsche

The friendly and flowing savage . . . Who is he?
Is he waiting for civilization or past it and mastering it?

—Walt Whitman

CONTENTS

IN REVERENCE

THE SOULS OF WHITE FOLK

—

ABUNDANT HEALTH AND LEISURE

—

IN REVERENCE

THE RAPE OF MAYBERRY

Mayberry is a town. It holds within itself the flesh and bones of a prayer, prayed as a formula requires. Mayberry is no different, in essence, from Thebes. It is a town, and to be a town is to be besieged. When the story of a town is told, the meaning of the story is to be found in the how of its being besieged, and in the arc of the town's response to that threat. In Aeschylus' *Seven Against Thebes*, the Chorus of Theban women, their city walls surrounded by hostile foreign soldiers, exclaim:

> I will try to do my part,
> to shape my prayer as these formulas require,
> but the pulse of fear will not be lullabyed;
> and in the neighboring regions of my heart
> anxieties ignite, terrors catch fire,
> and agitations, fanned by the blown sound
> of the circling hosts outside,
> smolder and burn. I quake,
> like the mild paralyzed dove who, from her perch,
> huddled with unfledged nestlings all around,
> eyes the thick snake.

What—or who—is Mayberry's snake? How does it approach Mayberry's citizenry? Who is Mayberry's mother-bird and what is her response to the snake? How do the unfledged nestlings, in Mayberry, cry out? In *Seven Against Thebes,* the threat is clear. The Chorus of women "stand in danger of slavery, rape, and death," and they say so. In Mayberry, the threat is seemingly less potent, and obviously more variable, while what is at stake—what the Sheriff means to safeguard and what the snake means to devour—is quite similar. Years of absorbing the story of this peculiarly American town—its walls, its ceaseless prayer—lead me to speculate about its place in the history of dream-towns. It seems to me that Mayberry manifests a new way to dream of tragic struggle. Conventional wisdom asserts that Mayberry is Eden, and so, a purely sentimental foolishness. But to watch the show carefully is to understand it is not an Eden; it is to understand that no storied place has ever been an Eden. If it *is* Eden, it is Eden with a snake in the grass, and when Eden's got a snake in the grass, it is already not-Eden. A story of Eden without a snake in the grass is a story without human meaning.

To ask about Mayberry's snake is difficult. In its many episodes, we encounter a wide range of seemingly unrelated threats. It is perhaps best to begin instead with a description of the town's walls. A snake, after all, has always taken its color and its shape from the walls it finds itself faced with, and it cannot be understood apart from those walls. Mayberry's snake certainly cannot be understood apart from Andy (the mild paralyzed dove) and the unfledged nestlings he broods over. One is tempted to oversimplify when one comes to this question—one is tempted to reduce the snake to *one* vague shape or category of shape—say, hubris, or laziness . . . just as one is tempted to settle on one superficial notion of what it is that Andy serves to protect: the weak, the innocent, etc. . . . We must resist these temptations and look more closely at the town and those who have, episode by episode, been made to move through it.

The Andy Griffith Show ran on CBS from 1960 through 1968. It never dropped below eighth place in the Nielsen rankings, and it was number one when it ceased production. It was not until episode 203 (201 in the order of filming), in the seventh season of production (just the second season to air in color) that The Andy Griffith Show dared to carry out into the open the sacred core of Mayberry: Bee Taylor's Deep Pink Ecstasy. I think it best to begin my analysis with this episode, this core.

The episode's story is a story founded upon Aunt Bee. Who is Aunt Bee? Aunt Bee has never married, never "been with" a man. She lives with Andy and Opie, her nephew and his son, and she mothers them. The woman Andy fucked, the woman who took in and gestated Andy's seed, is missing. She is not only missing—she is *altogether* missing. She is so missing that her being missing isn't ever mentioned; there are no words to signify her, her obscene role. In her place there is a virgin mother: Aunt Bee. The episode in question begins with Aunt Bee and her friends—Clara and Tillie—at a meeting of the Garden Club. The ladies sit and listen to the rules for this year's Hybrid Rose Contest. Clara, who has won the Contest seven years running, is overconfident, and she condescends to Bee when Bee reveals the name of her entry—Bee Taylor's Deep Pink Ecstasy. Clara remarks—and she is not wrong—that this is quite a pretentious name. Tillie sides with Clara; Tillie is the voice of reason, the voice of shameful assumptions.

The rest of the story unfolds as we would expect; there is bitterness between Bee and Clara/Tillie, Bee Taylor's Deep Pink Ecstasy is blooming perfectly—it is unspeakably beautiful—until it is accidentally destroyed by Opie the night before the Contest. When the grim morning of the Contest comes, Andy suggests that they should not go. He suggests that they should just go to Mount Pilot for a nice lunch . . . but Aunt Bee decides to do the decent thing. She attends the competition and watches sadly, but with intense pride, as Clara's rose is declared, yet again, the most beautiful. But wait. As Clara is about to walk up to accept her award, Opie arrives, and he has a photograph of what he destroyed. We have known all along, of course, that Andy took a photograph of Aunt Bee alongside *Bee Taylor's Deep Pink Ecstasy* before it was destroyed. It had not occurred to Andy or to Aunt Bee to have the photograph developed and to attempt to use it in the Contest, which is to say, to use it as a substitute for the rose itself. It had not even occurred to Opie; he was simply trying to make amends for the recklessness of his boyish play. It was fate and fate alone that allowed for the picture to arrive at exactly the right moment, wherein Clara was forced to see it. Clara, seeing the picture, is transfigured. She is moved to a powerful humility, and she declares that *Bee Taylor's Deep Pink Ecstasy,* though it does not exist, is the only rose truly deserving of the blue ribbon. The Judge concurs.

This would seem to be the end of the story. The rift between Bee and Clara is repaired and everyone in Mayberry senses that the best possible thing has happened. Bee and Clara sit together that evening on Bee's porch; they are the best of friends again, and they are recalling the precious youth they shared. They attended the same high school— Sweet Briar Normal—and played on the same high school basketball team. They compliment one another on their long-gone athletic abilities; Clara declares that Bee was the backbone of the team, and Bee declares that Clara was the best dribbler. This is where Andy comes in. His service to the town is not limited to protection; he also serves as the town's most trusted and capable witness. To protect and to witness cannot be understood as separate activities; to protect, Andy must know where he is, and how it stands with where he is. This witnessing is what Andy does, no less here than in episodes dominated by a suspicious Northern salesman. The scene closes not with a view of Bee and Clara, but with a view of Andy (the mild paralyzed dove) eavesdropping on his aged but still thoroughly unfledged nestlings. It would be easy to view this final scene as superfluous, but I don't think it is; in fact, I think this final scene provides the key for understanding the snake that means to devour Mayberry's citizenry.

Making his way to the porch with lemonade and cookies, Andy pauses to listen to the women singing their old alma mater's song:

> *Sweet Briar oh Sweet Briar*
> *Where hearts are young and gay*
> *Sweet Briar oh Sweet Briar*
> *Forever and a day*

He is moved. He witnesses something here—you can see it in his face. Has he witnessed his own town's Chorus of women, safe again from the snake that meant to devour them? Or has he witnessed the snake itself, the snake suddenly in the room, when it had just a moment before seemed so far away? There are several ways to imagine the snake in this episode. The snake is always a threat, a potential devastation arisen in the midst of the town. One could imagine it, then, in this episode, as the shameful pride that nearly overcomes the old virgins; or one could imagine it as the recklessness of boys at play. I don't think either of these is right. Neither of these *could be* to blame for the destruction of something so profound as a virgin-mother's deep pink ecstasy.

From the very start, and throughout the eight years of *The Andy Griffith Show,* the eight years of Mayberry's development, this was Mayberry's core unspeakable presumption: a virgin-mother's deep pink ecstasy. Aunt Bee is portrayed as, above all, a mother, but it is when we understand her as a *virgin-mother* that we begin to get at the tragic struggle that defines the town. *Bee Taylor's Deep Pink Ecstasy,* we need remind ourselves, is destroyed before she can enter into the glory it promised her; she is left with just a *picture* of her achievement. Her achievement, then, is not real—it is just an image. Her achievement is not different, in this respect, from her ongoing self: she is not, in reality, a mother. She is, from the very start, a substitute for the not-speakable real thing . . . which has always already been destroyed and has never had its destruction minded. Her being a virgin-mother signifies, above all else, the chasm that exists between the imaginary and the real. Virginity and motherhood are not separated by degree—they are *exclusive* of one another—just as the imaginary and the real share, in truth, nothing at all in common, and are forever exclusive of one another. It is the power of this exclusion, the power of this ever-widening chasm, that Mayberry means to harness.

This substitution of the imaginary for the real, in Mayberry, is not a strategy that is designed to hold off the snake; it is not a way of patching up holes in the wall. *It is the snake itself.* We learn this from, or through, Andy, the watchful mother-bird. In the final scene, he comes into an understanding; he understands that he is at home in a town of virgins and their children. The virgins have nothing but pictures of the reality they were once engaged with, and they mean to teach their children how to enter into having nothing but pictures—they mean to teach them how to be digested by that process *without incident.* Yes, their pictures are fading fast, but that only means that they are getting closer and closer to being completely settled. The deeper they sink into the belly of the snake, the more clearly they hear the words of the old alma mater, and the more able they are to believe that they believe in them.

Andy makes a lemonade toast at the end of the episode. It is a toast to Bee and Clara—two aged virgins glorying in a youth without incident. It is also a toast to Mayberry's having taken one more step toward being completely settled. Lastly, it is a toast to you, the viewer. You sit looking into a screen. You look into a picture of a man making a toast. *Here's to you,* he seems to say. *Here's to everyone there is who can't remember the last time he had the real thing.*

LETTERS FROM THE AMERICAN POET

October 27, 2003

Dear Joe,

I hope this letter finds you well. I'm writing to solicit you for a short piece for the next issue of *American Poet*. We're adding a new feature to the journal in which we'll have several authors writing short pieces on one topic—a semi-seminar—and would like you to be one of the authors in our premiere installment.

Some of my favorite authors, yourself included, seem to combine irreverence and sincerity in a way that only poetry can afford, and I would love to read your thoughts on it. Or, more directly, what are your definitions of and inclination toward irreverence?

The article, of course, can be of any tone that's comfortable to you. It can reference other authors or remain solely experiential—i.e. be as critical or personal as you like. In addition, we would like to include a poem by each of our authors, either new or reprinted.

We can offer you $250 for 750-1000 words, and our copy deadline is December 15th.

I sincerely hope this interests you. I think it could be

a fascinating read. Please let me know soon if you are able to accept this invitation.

Best Wishes,
American Poet

———

December 4, 2003

Joe,

The essay is great. Exactly the kinds of concerns I was hoping you'd address. I see why you worried about editing (censorship), and that's a pretty valid concern. The higher-ups 'round here can be (most often are) a bit squeamish. I'm going to be thinking of some things we can do to keep the awful from happening: a straight-up scalpel job. Some early ideas are: a special seal with a warning to the offendable marked-out words with a note to contact us if you would like the whole essay.

In the mean time, if you want to gather thoughts on what sort of editing you'd allow—or if you'd rather retract the piece in lieu of any changes—I'll be open to ideas.

Thanks again. Sorry to lure you into a subject and a publication that seem to be at odds. But how else will we change that?

All best,
American Poet

———

December 29, 2003

Joe,

We have plenty of time for revisions—at least until

the middle of January. We'll be pretty swamped here until after the holidays, so let's talk in the new year about the "FBI" document and/or any other solutions we can come up with in the holiday rattle.

American Poet

—

January 14, 2004

Joe,

I hope the road-trip was visionary. I have yet to confront the Authorities here with your essay, and am of a few minds about how to armor it. This is a wordy e-mail, so take a deep breath.

We could still go with the very obvious black marks—which might obfuscate the meaning of the sentences as well—or we could tone down the language (see below).

With any of these options, we would state very clearly that the piece has been censored, and that those interested in reading the uncensored version can contact me to have a photocopy mailed to them. We could even charge a fee, which we could send to you...

Here's a sample of a blackout paragraph:

"The apostles inquire about a rumor they've heard, a rumor which says that Jesus has --------------. Jesus deflects their questions with spiritual double-talk until ultimately the apostles force him to disrobe. It is discovered that Jesus has --------------------------- -------------------. Jesus, transfigured by his apostles' shock, initiates an orgy of sorts, --------------------- --."

Or the lower-contrast version:

"The apostles inquire about a rumor they've heard, a rumor which says that Jesus is not male. Jesus deflects their questions with spiritual double-talk until ultimately the apostles force him to disrobe. It is discovered that Jesus is not only not male, but female. Jesus, transfigured by his apostles' shock, initiates an orgy of sorts."

Also, I wonder how you feel about using 'pornography' instead of 'porn,' and what on earth we can do with the miraculous adjective "severally-penetrated."

Another possibility: Switch paragraphs 3, 4, and 5 with 6 & 7. In other words, locate the Illustration later in the piece so the piece builds up to it.

One more thing: we're including poems with each article, so if you have any new ones you think would look good with this—or any you'd like us to reprint—let me know.

All best in the new year,
American Poet

—

January 18, 2004

Joe,
The revisions are fantastic. I had read (and delighted in) the first revision, but will go with the second.

As far as the poem goes, it can either be one long or two short pieces, can be either prose or lineated poems, and can be either previously published or unpublished . . . whatever works best for you. If it's going to be a previously published one (or two), let me know so I can write off to whomever's permissions dept.

This is going to be great. I think you'll really like the Dean Young and Mary Ruefle pieces that complete the section.

Hope all's well,
American Poet

—

February 2, 2004

Joe,

I'm sorry I've taken so long to respond to your last e-mails. The long freeze up here has definitely affected us mentally.

I like the micro-poems & will be very glad to run them. If any of them have appeared elsewhere, let me know so we can acknowledge it.

I will definitely run by you the wording of any prefatory Censor's remarks and any actual mark-outs. I think these will be much fewer than we had originally discussed.

I'll be in touch. . . . hope, if you're teaching this semester, that it's a good class . . .

American Poet

—

February 22, 2004

j

Forgive my long silence, but I've been in a great struggle with the Authorities over here over your essay. I really don't know what to tell you at this point, except that if the piece is going to run it will have to be significantly edited.

I apologize profusely for getting you into this mess, as you have been one of the more forthcoming and flexible of the authors we've solicited.

If, at this point, you want to withdraw the piece, I definitely understand. I'll insist that the pay remain.

If, on the other hand, you want to re-work or re-imagine the piece, I'll stand by. If you're interested, it might help you to know that the other two pieces in the group are structured through fragmentary and stream-of-consciousness rather than rhetorical methods.

Of course, the real issue is the subject matter & the frankness with which you approach it that makes my bosses afraid to offend the elderly, wealthy people who make up our board and membership.

I fragmented your essay, removing controversial passages and, it seems, your entire point. To set up an analogical link between the Jesus figure and the pornographic actor through their shared bodily sacrifice was enlightening. I'm not sure my bosses even got that part. What stands in my chainsaw-edit is, of course, still interesting to me, but must insult you.

I apologize again for this extended uncertainty.

Give me a ring if you like, or an e-mail if you know what you would like to do at this point.

American Poet

—◁—

February 23, 2004

Joe,

I'm glad you still want to go forward with the piece even without its teeth. And I agree with you about keeping a notice about what's missing. I'm pretty certain that the piece will run as you returned it, but have not run it through all the alarmists. I'll keep you posted.

Thanks again,
American Poet

———

March 1, 2004

Dear Joe,

Bad, bad news. My boss has basically vetoed the article, and though I argued and argued (for weeks now, it seems) she is steadfast. She now claims that the article simply does not work, and no logic or rhetoric can convince her otherwise. What number of concerns are really behind this I do not know (to appear to be a censor was a big deal to her, even though cutting the entire article is of course an extreme form of censorship).

So we fought the law and the law won. I feel like an ass for all of this. I will definitely be sending you the check (paltry though it is). I hope that the process of writing the article made it at least somewhat worthwhile, and that you can submit it somewhere more adventurous and less organization-affiliated (ugh).

Once again, I wish I could offer a better explanation, but I feel like we're dealing with a decision that even its maker doesn't understand.

Keep up the fight,
American Poet

THE HOLY SPIRIT OF LIFE

The question of irreverence, of course, is the question of reverence. To revere . . . or to refuse to revere. . . . From the point of view of The Authorities, to refuse to revere is a dangerous thing, a thing to be punished. This kind of thing— the censor as a punisher—is not, however, what I want to talk about in this essay. Looking at the irreverence I am given credit for, I am struck by something more important.

I am struck by the reverence implicit in my alleged irreverences, and the reverence implicit, come to think of it, in many irreverences. Reverence is typically defined as: to fear something or to be in awe of something. The *of something* seems an afterthought, a given, such that one might consider excising it from the definition. But it's important; the act of reverence insists upon a profound separation of the Self from the revered Other's profound power. Poetic speech thrives on this separation. Poetic speech, I believe, is *always* reverent; when it is called irreverent, it has simply not been reverent toward the currently Authorized entities.

The reverences I came to practice in my own life were attached not to outlandish religious stories or grandiose philosophical notions but to physical facts: the ocean, the drinking of alcohol, fucking, the driving of cars, the playing of certain games/sports, the consumption of various drugs, the attendance of concerts. My poems tend to be in one way or another connected with (or profoundly disconnected from, i.e. lacking in) such instances of reverence. One poem I wrote last year can be traced back to the watching of pornography. In the pornography I've watched, there is sometimes a woman doubly or triply penetrated. I revere this woman. She confronts me with something; she forces me to know of something that I do not and cannot fully understand, but which somehow claims me.

The word obscene comes from tragedy, originally; there was an area off-scene, which is to say, off-stage, wherein a tragedy's unshowable but altogether decisive acts were imagined to have been carried out. The ob-scene was thus a pregnant silence looming up into the façade of the knowable story. The severally-penetrated woman on the T.V. is, for me, obscene in that sense; she is the transfigured façade, the façade saturated with an uncanny confluence of powers that I can feel but cannot possess, cannot reduce to narrative or to idea. The awe I feel is simultaneously ecstatic and terrible—awe*some* and aw*ful*. Its fact, to which I submit, is both humbling and empowering; in it, or with it, I am again a part of the mysterious undeniable ongoing real.

For me, the poetic is always just such a submission. It is reverence for the wrong thing, the thing that can't be accommodated. Such reverence finds itself treated with one of three fates. Fate one is for a poem to be mistaken for irreverence. (In the history of our particular brand of Authority, much poetry has suffered this sad fate. Celan's assertion—that it was his intention to blaspheme to the very last—can be taken, I think, as an expression of his devotion to the power of poetic speech in an age devoted—decidedly— to the imagination of less human powers.) Fate two is for a poem's reverence to go unrecognized, or to be ignored—to be judged incomprehensible. Fate three is for a poem to be engaged with properly, wherein the strangeness of authentic reverence is manifest.

When a poem suffers either of the first two fates— being called irreverent or being ignored—this is usually because it springs from and attempts to allow for a reverence that is difficult, complex, heterogeneous, and not reducible to the known. The function of such a reverence, moreover, is to admit a not-entirely-understandable situation, a situation we cannot wholly withstand but must nevertheless submit to. This is contrary to the function of Conventional reverence. In a culture such as ours, a culture increasingly dominated by Conventional reverence, poetic speech has become not so much criminal as unintelligible and/or irrelevant. This is not to say that reverences of the obscene are diminishing—if anything, they are growing by leaps and bounds. Popular reverences of the obscene, however, are milder, less intentional, easier to access and at the same time easier to conceal from ourselves; such reverences, unlike good poems, are less likely to create the sense that one has intentionally or meaningfully opposed the project of Conventional reverence. Poetic speech, when it is indeed poetic speech, is unique in how intentionally and how passionately it evokes a situation that cannot be resolved or entirely understood; for those in its thrall, this is precisely its charm, its distinctive ennobling transformation of attention.

I offer as an illustration the aforementioned pornography-related poem I wrote last year. In this poem I have Jesus talking with his apostles. The apostles inquire about a rumor they've heard, a rumor which says that Jesus has no dick. Jesus deflects their questions with spiritual double-talk until ultimately the apostles force him to disrobe. It is discovered then that Jesus has a "filthy cunt" where his dick ought to be. Transformed by his apostles' shock, Jesus furiously initiates an orgy of sorts, sucking their dicks and forcing them all to lick his "filthy cunt" and to fuck his ass.

In this little tale, I have inserted Jesus and his disciples into a porn scene. I did so intuitively, but on reflection, it was probably because the biblical Jesus stars in his own triple penetration scene (hand, hand, feet). Crucifixion was capital punishment designed for spectators—designed, that is, to fix the penetrated individual (penetrated above all by the heterogeneity that assures his own mortality) in a sensual spectacle, and a spectacle designed to demonstrate the depth of the power of a State. This spectacle, if we are to believe what Christians like Mel Gibson rather melodramatically assert, *was precisely what Jesus wanted*—it was the scene that his mission needed in order to come to its climax. Indeed, it is not unusual to find Christian theology that asserts that *the coming of Jesus* was not truly fulfilled until this moment—the decision to submit and to die being even more decisive than its result, the resurrection. Our savior only truly comes, then, via his public penetration, and, well, you can see why I was drawn to retelling the story so as to make it more realistic, more fitted to what I have understood as a possible avenue for reverence.

I have verified quite conclusively that the current Authorities (and those who gratefully abide them) consider this text of mine irreverent. For The Authorities, Jesus is the most reverence-worthy figure in all the world: beneficent heterosexual/asexual maleness. To assert Jesus as anything other than heterosexual/asexual maleness, and to situate profound power in a severally-penetrated individual is, in their view, to revere incorrectly. I understand the current rules of Conventional Reverence, and I chose to mock them, but I did not do so merely to have mocked them; the Jesus figure I assert is indeed worthy of reverence—much more worthy, in my judgment, than the Authorized Jesus figure. We must not, however, take the bait and approach such judgments as if they could be simply right or wrong. They are never right or wrong; they are always just the surprising gaudy health of the desire to seem more real.

Note: The essay above is the essay that was solicited and rejected by *American Poet*. It subsequently appeared in *Fence*. The piece it was written about, "Semiotics: Dehiscence Is Never/Always Sought," is included in the third section of this book. "Semiotics: Dehiscence Is Never/Always Sought" was submitted upon request to *Nerve.com*, whereupon it was enthusiastically accepted for publication, but subsequently rejected . . . due to an editor's fear of controversy. I neglected to archive the small string of emails I got from *Nerve.com*, as they were not imbued with much more than unselfconscious cowardice.

CRAZY

"The love that is not all pain is not all love."
—Antonio Porchia

I've always been drawn to pain-songs. I began as a teenager with what was in front of me, what was current (AC/DC, for instance), and as I got older I groped my way back toward an assumed origin, delving into Country and Blues both and getting a feel for where and how they diverged. I have come to suspect that there is in Country music a kind of pain-song that may be the key to understanding this divergence. The song of which I speak is the sort wherein a pain is conspicuously withheld, dammed by a melody that feels much too delicate to hold it back... but which nevertheless holds it back. Hearing this song, one feels a strain; the pain is not allowed, as in other kinds of blues, to manifest itself directly; instead, the pain is expressed by its own palpable absence, which is to say, by way of the strain upon its dam. To refine and amplify this strain is a strange decision—one might say a poetic decision, really, as it is the deliberate construction of a beautifully doomed façade.

The Louvin Brothers come to mind. Songs like,

"When I Stop Dreaming," and even Christian songs like "Satan Is Real." These songs are for me great examples of the thing I'm talking about. The song I'd like to examine in this essay, however, is *Crazy*, written by Willie Nelson. Like the aforementioned Louvin Brothers' songs, this song is, musically, a wonderful example of my subject. Its lyrics, moreover, are particularly demonstrative of my point.

> *Crazy...*
> *crazy for feeling so lonely....*
> *I'm crazy...*
> *crazy for feeling so blue....*

The song's first verses assert above all one thing: I am crazy—I am not sane—for I am in pain. The verses assert this, however, in a nonchalant manner, a manner seemingly free from pain. The aforementioned *for* is strange, and not only because of the manner in which it is sung. Its strangeness is a seed, and the next verses begin to grow the seed:

> *I knew...*
> *you'd love me...*
> *as long as you wanted...*
> *and then someday...*
> *you'd leave me*
> *for somebody new....*

We move on to an explanation of the pain, and it is, as Son House liked to point out, THE explanation of blues-oriented pain: trouble between a you and an I. What is relevant here, though, is that the pain is expressed in terms of the I's *knowing*—it is the fact that the I *knows* that is responsible for the distress, the rupture, in his world.

The second stanza, moreover, makes explicit the lover-beloved dyad. The you is obviously implied in the first stanza, but it is made explicit in the second; this explicitly manifest you is thrust into the role of a judge who has called into question the sanity of the I. We can hear the first stanza, that is, as though the I is just nonchalantly repeating what the you—who is a pronouncer of verdicts—has recently declared. *You are crazy* "for feeling so lonely." Loneliness, here, is the crime.

The I is judged to lack sanity because he is an I, and an I only—he is *lone*-ly. He has departed from the ground that is *ours*, the ground that implies sanity, which is always *our* sanity. How does he achieve such a departure? He becomes "so blue,"—he becomes overly forlorn—he enters too fully into the pain of knowing what must happen to every "you and I." Even so, he maintains his sane posture. He converses lazily in the direction of the absent beloved, and he seems almost to mock her as she overhears him. *I'm* crazy. . . . The I, from the very start, demonstrates a kind of self-possession that contradicts the intensity of sanity-destroying pain.

This self-possessing I is the miraculous dam I spoke of earlier—and the dam *sings,* the dam con-verses beautifully, even as it confesses that it is cracked, even as it withstands the pressure that gathers at that crack; the dam sings us a little song about the strain that *will* destroy it. We might ask why the I is this way—how he has become so ironic. Again, we need return to the knowledge that he has, or the knowledge that perhaps has him; this knowledge is also foreknowledge, and as such, it establishes the brevity of *every* "union" of lover and beloved (that is, past, present, and future), which is only ever "as long as you wanted."

The rupture, in this case, is not the I's fault—the I, in fact, seems to blame the you, whose desire wanes or changes direction. This particular you is a betrayer. The question then becomes: is another kind of you—a true you, let's say—really possible? I would say no; I would say that, even if we do take the blame seriously, the song is not merely about the possibility of one's running into a betrayer. No, the betrayal has opened up more essential knowledge having to do with the fate of every lover. The lover comes ultimately to understand that *something he did* couldn't even conceivably be the cause of such a deep pain, and he comes to understand, too, what love is—and is not—capable of.

> *I'm crazy...*
> *for thinking...*
> *that my love*
> *could hold you....*

He has here answered his own question—"why do I let myself worry?"—and in this answer we see that the problem is not circumstantial, but essential. The problem is with "love" itself and love's inherent inability to "hold you." That is, every lover has within himself a "someday" in which his beloved will be irretrievably lost. The arrival of this "someday" is at once the arrival of "somebody new," who can of course be understood as a new lover (a substitute for the I and the next victim for the act of love). We also can't help but hear the "somebody new" as the I himself, whose *new* identity—crazed loneliness—is the source of the song.

In the two lines that follow, this "new" I is summed up beautifully:

> *I'm crazy for trying...*
> *and I'm crazy for crying...*

The new I is paralyzed by the knowledge he has endured, and his unfolding of this knowledge has fixed us, his audience, in an abstract sense of love's impossibility. The song's last two lines proceed to wrench us out of that abstraction:

> *and I'm crazy for loving...*
> *you....*

The knowing I brings an end to his knowing by turning and for the first time acknowledging the presence of the *specific real* "you" that the song began for, the you whose specificity, whose reality, the song has not been able to diminish. This you, reappearing *no less loved* in the last moment of the song, vividly contradicts the alleged impossibility of love, even as it upholds the reality of the "trying" and the "crying" that the I finds himself paralyzed by. We come to understand, then, that the song itself—the formal addressing of the you—is the I's way out of the paralysis of knowing. With the song, the I is able to overcome, most of all, the paralysis that was brought on by what he knows; his singing produces, at first, abstract knowledge of the love process, but then dramatically asserts the limitation of that knowledge, which is the you itself, the reality that cannot ever really be reduced to abstraction. Thus, the foundation of love is defined as the irreducible impulse to imagine and dwell upon an unspeakably specific you. And while we do not know *which* unspeakably specific you the singer is singing of (first wife? second wife?), we do grasp *that* he is singing to an unspeakably specific you. We grasp this because we, too, as creatures of love, imagine and dwell upon such a you ourselves. Indeed, while the singer has lost *that* particular you, he, by way of singing, opens himself up to an other you, an other somebody new, and that is *you*, who has just now been made worthy of a song.

RESPECTING THE CHASM

For some time I've had a fantasy about having a studio in which to pursue my writing in some regular way. This is probably because I've read a lot about studios other writers have had. We seem to assume that each specific writer has specific circumstances in which his or her writing best unfolds. It follows that one's studio would be designed to maintain those circumstances. I don't know, though, if this assumption applies to me, my writing, because I've never had a studio, let alone any of the studios I've fantasized about.

Of course, circumstances do have an effect on my writing. I've noticed that certain situations lessen the chances that I will write, or write something of any worth. It's harder to pinpoint the inverse situations—the situations that could be said to increase my chances. Only the obvious things strike me: free time, proximity to a meaningful spectacle, freedom from looming hassles. I've been fortunate enough to get access to these things—now and then, and to some extent—but never to the extent that I felt I could take the next step, implementing a specific site and a specific ritual for the site. Instead, I've just written whenever I could, which means whenever a certain sort of quiet developed, the kind inclined to fill up with language that seems inexplicably telling. I've written, that is, wherever I could, which means alone at some table somewhere.

Thus, for me the really interesting question is: what are the underlying conditions wherein or whereby I am able to write poems? And my answer is: day-dream. I write poems from day-dream, which is the state or mood that obliterates the kind of sense that registers specific locale. Day-dream space is illocal, to use a Dickinsonian term—it is wherein my ordinary sense of where I am is no longer operative.

Gertrude Stein said: "It takes a lot of time to be a genius. You have to sit around so much doing nothing, really doing nothing." I'd argue that Stein, here, is speaking of the day-dream, the quiet, that I'm speaking of. Its origin is mysterious, to say the least. It has to do with extracting oneself from doing something, if by doing something one means being immersed in a self-possessed, heard-of activity; to be extracted from heard-of activity is at the same time to be extracted from being somewhere, if by somewhere one means some previously inhabited place. Such extraction allows for a quite different sense of things to develop, and out of this sense a kind of profound inaction might take place.

Most mysterious in this whole process is the final step in the extraction, the going from being *near* day-dream to being *in* day-dream. I'd like to compare this transition with the transition that a sleeper experiences as he goes from waking thoughts to asleep thoughts (i.e. dreaming); in a way, it is not a knowable step—it is perceptible only by implication, when it's long gone, and even then only within a kind of guesswork. Its having taken place is known because of what it has produced: the dream, the poem. To compare poem-generating-space to dream-space is hardly original. Recent discoveries about sleep, however, have enriched the analogy considerably.

We now know, for instance, that the brain needs sleep; we don't know exactly why, but we do know that we cannot *live* without it. We can go without sleep for only about as long as we can go without food. Our need of poetic speech is not such that we will die if we do not have access to it, but there can be said to be an inherent need of it or an inclination toward it. The analogy is even stronger on other points. For instance, consider that in sleep, the brain shuts down, above all, its attention and memory functions. The sleeper closes his eyes and literally ceases to know where he is; he is released from his ordinary (i.e. sensually verified) notion of location. Dream space, because it is purely imaginary, is illocal, and thoroughly believed in.

The key point is that the dreamer is freed from the diminished reality implicit in attention, and freed from the kind of memory that works for and within attention's necessary vanity. Imagination, during sleep, is able to derive imaginary coherences typically too large—too broad, too subtle—for attention to make useful. Images detached from the locus of "reality" turn more clearly and easily to one another, even as they are driven to seek what they lack, leading the dreamer always back toward the reality he has never been able to fully represent. Hearing poems, or recalling dreams while we are awake, we stand strangely between our two potential modes for regarding reality: we stand at attention, which possesses and thereby diminishes reality, and at the same time we bear witness to imagery that, because it is evocative of a less diminished reality, is capable of possessing us.

I've written poems because I've had the sense that attention can diminish reality. In writing poems I allow images to be detached from their false foundation, which is to say, from the ordinarily and easily possessed reality (with all of its common sense); thus detached, the images might turn to one another more carefully, more ambiguously. In doing so, they provide, in the best-case scenario, a glimpse of a less diminished reality, which I am happy to be possessed by. And I mean happy mainly the way that one is happy to scream or punch a wall when one feels an intense despair or frustration. Good poems, in my view, are joyful cruel sabotage, and I must confess that I enjoy their obliteration of the diminished reality as much as their glimpse of what withstands that obliteration. The process is highly emotional; both the trigger and the response it produces, so long as they remain true, resist being organized or devised. To be concerned about the concrete location of the process (i.e. the studio)—the kind of space it lives to obliterate—seems odd to me. It presumes, I think, that the chasm between what we say and where we are can be understood, managed, or even lastingly bound together. I find fault with this presumption; it disrespects the chasm.

LAVING THE CHUFF

I've decided that all of my writing from this point forward shall stem from one phrase, a phrase which I feel is the ecstatic culmination of all my years of struggle in the writing "field," and that phrase—utterly original in my view—is: laving the chuff.

All other phrases pale in comparison with this new-found ROCK, upon which I shall now build: LAVING THE CHUFF.

I am lucky to have found such a phrase; I certainly do not deserve it and I do not have the proper childhood traumas in place to assert that it could only have come into the world via me, my shaky voice. I will be satisfied to call myself lucky, and to continue to glory in the miraculous ring of the wondrous thing I have found: *laving the chuff.*

But what does it MEAN, I can hear you cry out? My first impulse is to insist that whoever has asked that question has just given himself away: he could not have heard me. And I know that I did not stutter. I said, "laving the chuff," and anyone present had every opportunity to hear—as clearly as a bell or an honest cry of pain—my full meaning. The most miraculous thing about the phrase (and I cringe every time I use this term, "phrase," to refer to my most sacred act, my most solemn event) is that, even if one does not know what "laving" means, and likewise does not know what "chuff" means, one can easily understand them when they are taken together: laving the chuff.

Each word—alone—may remain shrouded in darkness, but when placed next to the other, the totality of their meaning becomes quite clear. One begins to understand laving because one understands that it must be performed upon the chuff, and one begins to understand the chuff because one understands that it is what allows for or even insists upon laving. "Error in logic!" cry the nervous citizenry of the settled world. And still, they have heard me, and they have entered already into the splendid new house that I have built: laving the chuff.

Where do I go from here? Repeat myself—repeat myself only? Be content with myself as a one-hit wonder? That would not be so bad. Laving the chuff, I am certain, will stand the test of time, every day luring in new witnesses and surprising the old ones with how cleanly it evades redundancy. But perhaps I will endeavor to build upon my good fortune; perhaps I will allow myself to be drawn in to pursuing all the implicit potentials in what I have found: laving the chuff.

For example, one day I had the impulse to add the word "just," creating: just laving the chuff. (A variation on this is to use the word jes', which perhaps applies the blackface it verges on: jes' lavin' the chuff.) I know that every addition diminishes the core components and their radiant affinity for one another—even so, I feel that I learn something from each experiment. With the variations I've imagined, that is, I may not have created equal entities, but I have plumbed my own mood-process, which is relevant, given that I am not always (or not even often) ready for embracing the maximum radiance of laving the chuff. In my day-to-day life I am most often dimmed, and dimming, and not up to the fullness of my own simple achievement.

Because I myself am a chuff-laver. Do you see? Besides dimming the core radiance, variations create new perspectives, which means varying degrees and kinds of involvement in the event. Variations are like a murderer's denials—no matter how long he talks, his talk will never ascend to the unspeakable moment in which he has done what he has done . . . but that talk may provide, over time, myriad smaller senses of why he did it, or how he has gone on with himself since. The laving of the chuff. The chuff, laved. Lave the chuff, baby!

One's day is full of births, deaths, and all the tragi-comic devotions of what there is between. Some of these devotions are mere seconds long, some go on for hours, and some go on for years. But however long they are, the fact remains: we drift *into* them and then *out of* them. Sometimes quickly, sometimes so slowly we fall asleep on the way. And for every moment in that process—for every moment in our moving all at once into and out of our countless devotions—there is a variation of laving the chuff that is appropriate. One just has to look within, where the chuff is undoubtedly laven.

IN RESPONSE TO THE DISCIPLINARY ACTION TAKEN AGAINST ME BY THE HUMAN RESOURCE MANAGER

Dear Human Resource Manager:

When you use the word *human* to refer to me, I don't know what you mean. You assume, I think, that human says *what I am,* but actually this word, used here as a noun (you call yourself a *Manager of Humans*), is vague and misleading. For too long, you and people like you have used this simple signifier to signify an incredibly complex part of reality. Originally, which is to say, as far back as the Latin (as far as we can well trace it), it comes from the Latin word *humus,* which meant "earth." Latin *humanus* meant "earthly being."

In time, humanus came to take a different definition; the human, or human *being,* came to be understood as a "rational" "animal." Within this new conception, being and earth were no longer referenced, at least not directly or in any way that could claim an understanding of being or of earth. I might accept your referring to me as an earthly being, but I do not accept your assumption of me as a rational animal; who I am is not determined by my animal status . . . nor my ability to think within the confines of rationality.

By defining me as essentially a rational animal, you misrepresent me, and I believe you do so—or the tradition you numbly carry forward does so—intentionally. That is, by creating this idea of "the human," your tradition creates an identity that is more substance than stance, more a fixed nature than a site wherein unfixed and always evolving natures are fucking colliding. My identity, if I must choose *one,* is not substantial; it is not a "stuff" of one or another kind. My identity, let us say, is not a party-goer; it is the party itself.

The last two terms in the title that you claim for yourself tell the whole story. You are the *Manager* of a *Resource.* The human, for you, is a resource, which means a substance, and like all substances, it has certain properties. If you are able to understand these properties, you are able to make that substance useful. Your Management skills are, at bottom, your ability to seize upon these potential usefulnesses. Let me say again to you that I am not such a substance. Moreover, even if I was such a substance, I do not believe you when you say that you have the best interests of this substance at heart. I will go even further and suggest that you are not even capable of telling me *toward what end are you managing the human substance?* Before we proceed in our relationship, I would like you to answer that question for me. Please be specific in your answer.

Before I address your ability to manage me, I would like you to show me that you have an answer for that question. What are you, as Manager, using the human substance for? What is your goal for yourself, the user? What is your goal for the substance that is being managed? Folks manage hogs toward slaughter, and so, toward they own dinner; folks manage poppy plants for opium, and so, for they own pleasure—but why do you manage me? What can you bring to me or to the world itself that is not already present and secure? It is my suspicion that in truth you have nothing whatsoever to offer, and that the "Manager" position you occupy exists as the direct result of a specific recent history. That history is a history of organized and massive brute-force and the armed occupation that always follows. It is also my suspicion that, as this occupation wears on, its brute force, as it becomes less and less apparent, becomes all the more despicable and foreign to us, the few on-earth beings not yet dissolved under its weird vague hope.

Yours Sincerely,
Joe Wenderoth

PERSONALITY

Technology, they say, is changing the "nature" of "human" "experience." Indeed. I would like to see it do so in more amusing ways. What if we were to introduce into our diet a chemical that causes even the slightest traces of piss to emanate a neon orange glow. This would mean that our hands and our clothes would often—just how often would be the mind-boggling thing—have a piss-glow. Gas-station "rest-rooms" would glow so deeply and thoroughly that entering into them would be like entering into dream-space. Candy bowls on the counters of Diners—always tinged with a piss-glow. Soon we would come to understand ourselves differently—we would be the always pissing, piss-cleaning, piss-covered, piss-drenched thing. We would be the natural (which is to say, mindless) gatherer of that glow. The flow and the glow of selves would be clearly parallel to the flow and the glow of piss, and we would struggle in one, the other, or both directions. Our inability to establish complete control over said flows would glow—neon orange—and we might learn to accept that glow as our very own. Such acceptance would become either celebration or the dignity of rugged endurance, and in many cases we would not be able to say which. Concurrently, of course, there would always be the mainstream, those who struggle nervously to lack in the glow, and achieve, here and there, that lack.

THE SOULS OF WHITE FOLK

In 1999 I moved to Marshall, Minnesota to teach in the English Department at what was then called Southwest State University (SSU). SSU was a small public liberal arts college; the population of the town of Marshall was around twelve thousand and of this number some three thousand were at the University. The great majority of students were from the surrounding rural counties of Minnesota and South Dakota; the majority were first generation college students. Thus, a college town, but an unusually isolated college town in rural southwest Minnesota. The closest metropolitan area was Sioux Falls, South Dakota, a good hour and a half drive. The weather contributed even more to the feeling of dramatic exile; strong prairie winds and bitter cold in the winter, stifling heat in the summer.

The essays that follow are some of the evidences of my time in the so-called American heartland (bitter cold, strong winds, heavy-set white people); they are more explicitly political than the other essays in this book. For me, just residing in Marshall was a kind of political activism, and perhaps the best kind: largely spontaneous and uncontrived. To be lodged in such a decidedly conservative place, I found, was to be lodged in a kind of expectation, the expectation of conservation itself. What was to be conserved? The American Way. What is the American Way? The American Way is simply what America began as, and what it has attempted (usually successfully) to "conserve" itself as: capitalist, white supremacist, homophobic, Christian-privileging patriarchy. Obviously, strides have been made in the struggle to change this Way, but I am always struck—and was especially struck in rural Minnesota—by how easily the "conservative" instinct is able to recover its vigorous pride and re-apply its core assumptions to whatever "issue" was current.

Living in Marshall, I became keenly aware that lived life—not just some set of political issues—was at stake. I watched as the University debated the rights of Christian fundamentalists; are they free to use public space to harass gays and lesbians with threats of eternal damnation? When the U.S. invaded Iraq on false pretenses, I listened to the gleeful hate-speech of insecure white men in bars; the looks on their faces reminded me of the gleeful faces one sees in pictures of lynchings. And I took note of how resigned to fearful silence were the great majority of the people who knew better. I myself drifted in and out of shameful silences. What I did get written—and usually published in the local newspaper or the campus newspaper—is here below.

THE SOULS OF WHITE FOLK

I think it's time to transform our image of Martin Luther King Jr. It's time that all likenesses of him became white. He was a wonderful selfless guy, passionately devoted to helping oppressed others. And he was struck down, tragically martyred—what more could anyone have asked of him? He was, in his lifetime, much despised by many people, and this hatred was profound because it came largely from whites, who held all the power. Once he was killed, it became easier for his oppressors to transform him—to gradually take him in, even. We've progressed to the point where much of the country celebrates (or at least tolerates the celebration of) Martin Luther King Jr. Day. It's not all that unusual, I will even venture to say, to find white Americans who claim to admire him.

But is this admiration enough—why not something more powerful? Why not *love?* And what of the many whites who, snickering, condescend to *tolerate* the celebration? And what of the many whites who still dislike and are made uncomfortable by the Reverend King, or even openly confess to *hating* him? I say it's time we make him white. If we make him white, we'll make it easier for both admiring *and* snickeringly tolerant whites to love him, and for hateful whites to take the first step toward condescending tolerance. And blacks will understand the revision; it's all in the name of progress, after all—it's all in the name of increasing the de facto stature of a great man. Wasn't it King who pointed out that it was *not* the color of the skin that mattered? Wasn't it King who insisted that one should be judged without concern for the color of one's skin? Poetic justice, then, to refashion him white, if only as a demonstration of the irrelevance of skin color. Moreover, to make him white would carry on King's practice of Christian compassion, in that it would make it easier on those folks who have a hard time accepting his current image.

Which brings me to the real inspiration for my idea: Jesus. Jesus, in actual fact, did not look like these pictures and statues we see all over the place. We know, for certain and without any doubt, that he would not have appeared white; and yet, growing up, I *knew* that he was white; every picture I encountered portrayed him as decidedly white. He is always long, angular, smooth-skinned, and pale; he is never short, broad, hairy, and dark. Insert a short, broad, hairy dark man into our typical representations of Jesus . . . and we have a problem.

Obviously, the two situations—Jesus and King—are on some levels not comparable. The revisers of the Jesus image had an easier task; there were no photographs and no videos to contradict, and there has been a great deal more time. I suppose one might argue that I am rushing things, and that King will attain to whiteness in his own time, over centuries. But that isn't the point.

The point is: King and Jesus are similar in another more important way. King claimed to be a follower of Jesus, in fact, and the struggle he immersed himself in was a struggle akin to the struggle the historical Jesus engaged in. Both struggled for the oppressed—struggled, that is, against a *specific* dominant group, which we might well call the oppressors, the elite, the wealthy, the owners, the well-off—and this struggle evidenced a kind of love for a specific sector of the oppressed. But to love a specific oppressed group can be (and certainly was, at least in King's and in Jesus' cases) problematic; the way in which these men endeavored to love a specific group was not only to indict the specific dominance that was in place in the given age—it was also to indict the concept and the apparatus of dominance itself. King with his marches and his demands to admit blacks into white Universities, *as if an oppression-free world (poverty-free, prejudice-free) would soon take root and blossom.* And Jesus with his eye of the needle threats and his harassment of the money-changers, *as if a New Kingdom (again, oppression-free, even to the point of the earth being inherited by the meek) would take root and blossom.*

We now understand—well, any securely middle-class patriotic American now understands—how woefully naïve is this kind of love. We now understand that it is the fault of the poor and oppressed that they are poor and oppressed—it is by way of their own poor decisions (no pun intended) that they do not attain to middle-class luxury. One hesitates to say that it is the *sin* of the poor that makes them what they are, but this hesitation is probably due to *our* decency, *our* patience with their sorry, tragic lives. And our decency, our patience, in the face of *their* irresponsibility, is at last waning, which is why we nearly elected, and then did elect, George W. Bush. Mr. Bush understands that to love the poor and oppressed *as though it was not their fault that they were poor and oppressed . . .* is not as malicious as it is simply naïve. And this naïveté can, in King's case as well as Jesus' case, be repaired. We have repaired it in Jesus' case by transforming him into a wonderfully ahistorical creature, a super-man in a distant world that has no significant connection to our own world. King's nonwhiteness, while we should admit that it was necessary at the time of his life, has now become an impediment to a full appreciation of him. The sooner we revise his image and afford him with whiteness, the sooner we will allow him to be loved as fully as he deserves.

It will not be easy; the current image of King as conspicuously black has saturated our society. We will have to go very gradually, making him lighter and lighter each year. And it won't be merely skin color we will have to deal with—his features, his voice, his way of moving, the nature of his concerns—all of these will need to be interrogated and altered so as to seem completely worthy of whiteness. We have the technology, as they say, and we can rebuild him. Even twenty years ago, the task would have seemed unworkable, but now, since we have parted more decisively with our naïveté about so many things, we have the resolve and the technology to get the project underway.

We need only to keep in mind the essence of our challenge: to remove from the King story the actual circumstances of the historical period—to remove, that is, the apparatus of dominance and the specifics with which that dominance was manifest (i.e. in this case, the whole white and black thing). We need to say: "all of that is behind us now." It would be instructive, at this point, to take again as our example Jesus' concern for others—actual specific others in history—and see how that concern was transformed, and made more useful, by generations upon generations of Christians. After much noble work, these Christians were able to transform Jesus' concern for *others* into a concern for *them,* that is, a concern for each Christian individual's *own personal* salvation. There are those who argue that this transformation is blatantly selfish—that it absurdly warps the whole of Jesus' teaching (i.e. his insistence on his followers' setting aside their own welfare and tending to actual others). We need only point out to these sad liberal types that the world has changed, and that our new world is nothing at all like any of those old worlds. Racism, for instance, was at one time somewhat common, whereas now it has been so thoroughly overcome that reverse discrimination is now a more significant issue. Again: "all of that is behind us now."

In the new age—let us call it *The Age Of Tremendous Freedom*—oppression is at an end. Thus, to saddle someone we care about with anything less than the most positive image . . . is careless. I don't mean to blame anyone for King's actual appearance—how could I?—but I would like to blame those who are not willing to step in and revise that image in a way that will bring more respect to the great man. To these folks I would say, "So what he was considered a black man his whole life? What have you got against freedom?"

FUCK-SOUNDS IN THE CLASSROOM

I sat in recently on a Soul music class. How strange it is to listen to SOUL music in that kind of public setting. Paralyzed, drug-and-alcohol-free, asexual, sterile, grim laboratory, that is. And I don't mean Minnesota—I mean the auditorium that the class was held in. This is not where Soul music—not where any great music—comes from or makes itself known.

You have to put music into its life-context to grasp it fully. It is always celebration and/or a grieving, and either way, it's a definite departure from our everyday stance. We are often—just how often is the surprising thing—READY for such a departure. The body wants to dance, stamp, thrust, sway, rock, fuck.

As celebration, music is desire—it is the seeking of pleasure via rhythm. As such, its public manifestation is our getting blended into a scene wherein pleasure is sought in many ways simultaneously: sex, dance, drugs, etc. . . . Where is the penultimate place to go to FEEL what Soul music—what any great music—is, and is for? The jukejoint, the honkytonk, the club. You know the names of the places in your neck of the woods, and one takes what one can get.

The other dominant avenue for celebration and/or

grieving—that is, for getting OUT of one's everyday stance—is the religious tradition. Whatever culture we look at, no matter how far back we look, we see that "holy" spaces and religious traditions have provided an outlet for celebration and/or grief. With Soul music we see this clearly in the presence and tradition of black churches. Sam Cooke began as a gospel singer, as did Aretha, who was the Reverend's daughter, and on and on.

In either case—at the bar or at the church, high or sober—a kind of ecstasy is sought. Ek-static—the word's etymology is ek (out) static (standing). To out-stand, to stand out. But to stand out from what? To stand out from the groove, to stand out from the rut of one's everydayness. To stand out from it, and then to drive back down—desperately—INTO it. To thrust into and out of the groove—into and out of, into and out of, oh FUNK ME!

Great Country music is identical to great Soul music in its function, which is to produce and inhabit the ecstasy that is possible in grief and/or celebration. Because of the age-old tradition of American racism, Americans think that there is a huge difference between "black" music and "white" music, as if the segregation of white and black has in actual fact—in lived life—been achieved. But great "white" music and great "black" music have always fed off of one another in this country, and in truth they vary only in the way that fucking varies—fast, slow, with this rhythm, with that rhythm. Fucking remains fucking, white or black, and fucking has been, more often than we are permitted to admit, white AND black. And fucking simply feels good; it produces a cry-call-howl-yowl-shout, which the body feels itself trying to get hold of. The body learns, via this noble doomed effort to get hold of ecstasy, that it can know, for whole moments at a time, what success means.

Ray Charles loved Country music and recorded many Country songs. I have heard people say this is odd, but it's not odd at all. He takes beautiful sad rhythmic Country yowls and he makes them even more ecstatic by infusing the sort of gently orgasmic swing that Soul music is so much defined by. I recommend his Country albums. And when you listen to them, listen for the orgasms. Even in a classroom—even in a laboratory—you can hear when he comes.

REGARDING THE CAMPUS EVANGELISTS

If I would have known that you would behave in this way,
I would not have shown you my gods.
—The Emperor Montezuma, speaking to Cortes

There is a poster around campus these days—one of many advertising Christian groups—that pictures a shield. Within the shield, in bold letters, there is the word: TRUTH. A large "1" is beneath the word, and in smaller letters there is written: *campus ministry.* I am a great fan of truth, especially the emboldened capitalized kind, and so I was drawn to the ad. But why the "1" beneath it? I was puzzled. Truth is a tremendously complex and difficult-to-grasp thing, while the number "1" is so simple and easy to understand—what's the connection? I read on to the smaller print at the bottom of the ad: "Salvation is to be found through him alone; in all the world there is no one else whom God has given who can save us. Acts 4:12." And then, as if one such pronouncement was not enough, there was another: "I am the way and the truth and the life. No one comes to the Father except through me. John 14:6." Now I got it. Now I understood the cleverly devised shield: *one truth.* There is just one truth, and it is possessed by the campus ministry. Some questions arose:

who the fuck is the campus ministry, and what gives them the right to tell me how I can and cannot be saved? These are, in essence, the questions that Montezuma put to Cortes, and it might be argued that Christian missionaries have never answered them in any satisfactory way.

As the *Campus Crusade For Christ* and other similar groups take to increasing their harassment of the unsaved on campus, I object—I wonder publicly if it is necessary to endure this kind of harassment. By wondering in this way, I have aroused further self-righteousness, albeit the more "Constitutional" kind. I was told that I was trampling "the rights" of these poor people by suggesting that I might not be required to endure their harassment. Well, it is absurd to suggest that "the rights" of Christians in this country or on this campus are or ever have been endangered. Christians in America, historically speaking, have never been the ones whose "rights" have been endangered—no, Christians have been the ones who have endangered the rights (and the lives) of others.

Historically, the Christian "approach" to other world-views has been to: a) condemn them as, at best, "lost," and at worst, as "worthy of execution"; b) vilify them as evil cults (pseudo-religions) designed to lure souls away from "the one true way"; c) condescend to them in order to "save" them from their own inherent lack of culture and personal dignity. In this respect, Christians have accurately reflected the psyche of the average American citizen—indeed, one could argue that Christianity has served as the necessary core, the necessary validation tool, of America's white supremacist patriarchal history. God bless America.

The history here cannot be argued—it is not subtle. Condemnation, vilification, condescension—a vigorous and prolonged discouraging of "foreign" or "unchristian" world-views. And one would need to be quite blind and even more dim to fail to grasp that this history is still with us.

Yes, thankfully, it has changed a bit. The condemnations today are less publicly celebrated, and the vilifications are less direct, and even less vicious in most cases. The condescension, however, seems to have increased, or at least to have increased in the variety of methods it might employ; Christian energy, deprived of its condemnation/vilification outlets, has blossomed into wondrous new strategies for stooping to conquer the sad diversity of the world's views (a/k/a "lost souls"). This is, as I said, an improvement. To endure the pity—and the pity only—of the true believers . . . is something I can live with.

Right-wing Christians often frame the issue of their harassing others in terms of "the rights" of individuals to believe what they want to believe; they do so because they are lodged in a history of extreme privilege, and this lodging causes them, when confronted with any kind of resistance, to turn immediately toward their own "inalienable rights." The issue, however, is not an individual's right to practice this or that religion (unless of course said religion proposes to use unchristian substances, or to engage in unchristian ceremonies or kinds of society)—the issue is *a group's* right to advertise, in the halls of a State University (i.e. a University founded upon the notion that all religions are equally welcome and worthy of respect), its own religion as *the only* dignified way to live. . . . SSU is a public liberal arts University that, in its mission statement, declares its commitment to promoting diversity; in such an institution, should one group have the right to create an atmosphere of open disrespect for all worldviews that are not its own? Should the campus of a University that is devoted to the objective treatment of facts and to the appreciation of the world's diversity and complexity—should such a campus allow any one group to promote opposition to diversity, complexity, and objectivity?

Imagine what would happen if a fundamentalist Islamic group began to promote itself in SSU's hallways with the vigor of the *Campus Crusade For Christ*. Imagine all the wonderful posters—"only Allah saves!" and "Mohammed is your only true friend"—and imagine if this group *had some success* in recruiting students into its long-overdue straightforward mind-set. Imagine, next, the outcry from the community, from parents fearful for the safety of their children! The fact is, there would be hysterical objection to this group, and to any fundamentalist group setting up shop on campus . . . *unless that group happened to be Christian.* Christians, in this country, get an exemption. Even the most ludicrous elitist Christian sects (growing by the day, it seems) are tolerated in a way that other groups are not, and this because . . . *they are us,* while the others are not us.

That said, I do not support a ban on religious clubs of any sort, even when they stand in opposition to the University's mission and to learning itself. It might be nice, though, if the University could develop a policy to limit and specify the walls on which the various groups might harangue the lost souls; this way, on days when one was feeling lost, one could walk thoughtfully through those hallways. We could even call those hallways: "the halls of the lost souls." I can't help but think how nice it would be to walk through *the other* hallways, the ones without signs constantly reminding me of how much I, as a caretaker of the learning process, am up against. How nice it would be to think that feeling lost, or even *being* lost, was not a bad thing—not a thing to be conquered—but instead was just the thing that motivated students and teachers to keep coming back to class.

TWENTY-FIVE WAYS TO MAKE LOVE
WITHOUT HAVING SEX

1. Give a blow-job.
2. Give a bare-ass spanking.
3. Nibble your partner's nipples.
4. Try a dildo in your own ass as your partner watches.
5. Try a dildo in your partner's ass.
6. Eat your partner out.
7. Put your fingers up your partner's ass.
8. Titty-fuck her.
9. Give his testicles a tongue-bath.
10. Rub your clit while he watches.
11. Lick your partner's mouth.
12. Sit on your partner's face.
13. Jerk off onto your partner.
14. Jerk off on yourself as your partner watches.
15. Watch some porn together.

16. Make up a secret language to describe the porn you've watched together.

17. Spank yourself as your partner spanks his or herself.

18. Rub your nose on your partner's clit.

19. Give a rim-job while your partner masturbates.

20. Squeeze her breasts from behind while your cock-head nuzzles up to her lubricated asshole.

21. Suck your partner's earlobe.

22. Try heavy petting while he or she pretends to be dead.

23. Give a hand-job.

24. Slap your partner's face with your titties.

25. Go with your partner to see naked others in public and talk about and with each naked other encountered.

BRINGING FREAKS TO CAMPUS

We are all freaks, yes. That is to say, each of us has moved through a bizarrely particular—and to some degree unique—set of circumstances, and now here we are. Life itself is, among other things, a series of freak shows, and I encourage you, gentle reader, to enjoy these shows without shame or hesitation. That said, when a former participant in MTV's "The Real World" came to speak at the University I worked for, I was disturbed. When, soon after this "talk," the father of a Columbine victim came to speak about the importance of faith in Jesus, I was more disturbed. This latter show, I was told, sold out the gymnasium, and the campus newspaper described it as *inspiring for everyone* in attendance. I am not sure it is the best thing for a University's students to use the funds provided for them by the University . . . to set up Freak Shows. Funds are limited, after all, and the task of a student fortunate enough to attend the University is not to gain exposure to more freakish freaks than he has access to in his hometown or in his dorm.

The task of a student fortunate enough to attend the University is to learn. In order to learn, one studies—one hears lectures—within the various disciplines. These lectures are delivered by persons who have devoted themselves to their given discipline and to knowing about and through it. While such lectures will no doubt be delivered by freaks... that freakishness is not the subject of the lecture, and that freakishness has nothing whatsoever to do with the discipline or the knowing that the discipline has brought about. That is, during such lectures, the freak's freakishness is not on display—it is bracketed, and irrelevant, or it should be (and can be), and we the audience look not into freakishness but into the various possibilities of knowing.

There are countless victims in the world—countless victims of countless bizarre developments. Some such developments are reckoned to be "positive"—being chosen to appear, for instance, on "The Real World." Some such developments are horrific; these produce the sort of freaks we feel sorry for—the freaks we sympathize with, because we know their story could easily be ours. Columbine was one such tragedy; Columbine has become notable in the American media not because it was a particularly massive or meaningful tragedy, but because it involved a predominantly white school in a middle-class neighborhood, and because the tragedies it manifested came all at once instead of one by one. Many more nonwhite non-middle-class children are killed—like clockwork—on the streets of American ghettos, and it's not big news at all. While we should obviously be concerned for the victims of Columbine, we should also be concerned about asking the question: why is the safety of children only an issue for this or that kind of neighborhood? In any case, and whatever the tragedy, it is not a good thing to shun its victims, or to try to avoid them, their awkward hurt presence, should they cross your path. No, you should tend to them, hear them out, help them through. But an altogether other question is: *should we seek these people out* when they don't cross our path, and should we invite them, thereby, to speak within the context of a University?

Let's say someone is crushed—paralyzed—by an

avalanche. Should we have him come and speak about "his sense" of geological processes? Unless he happens to be a geologist as well as an avalanche victim . . . of course we shouldn't. If he is not a geologist, his experience is NOT going to produce a larger understanding of what happened to him. No, the only thing it will produce is a vivid sense of his freakishness: *come and listen to me because I was actually crushed by an avalanche!* Perhaps this particular avalanche victim believes in Magical Dwarves; perhaps he believes, moreover, that avalanches are caused by Magical Dwarves, who he has perhaps offended by failing to touch his own forehead in the proper way or by failing to develop a "personal relationship" with one or another of said Dwarves. What we have here is nothing new to human history; what we have here is a freak who has taken to self-righteously mining his own freakishness for a larger understanding of the universe. When students at a University are eager to attend the performance of such a freak—a freak who has taken to mystically mining his own freakishness for "deeper insights" into his condition—it might be said that the University has failed to awaken in students an understanding of their real task.

Please believe me when I tell you that I am not against freak shows—and not even necessarily against self-righteous superstitious freak shows. I simply think we have enough of them on the Maury Show and at the Mall of America and just about everywhere else there is. The University should be different; it should be a refuge from Freak Shows. It should be the place wherein we refrain from tickling ourselves with the freakishness of freaks. It should be the place where we tend passionately to the dignified processes of knowing.

THIS TRYING NOT TO TELL THE STORY

These last few days since the terrorist attack on the World Trade Centers and the Pentagon, I find myself thinking mostly of those unlucky passengers, for they have now experienced what is perhaps my worst nightmare. Though nothing in my own experience is comparable to what they suffered, I think I (and I think many of us, especially those of us who have a strong fear of heights, a strong fear of falling out of the sky) have a pretty keen sense of at least *the kind* of horror they had forced upon them, and forced upon them to the utmost. One naturally and rightly feels intense anger toward those who immerse others in such a horror. In this case, though, the anger, if we are honest about it, is difficult to hold on to—it seems immediately subsumed or transfigured by the strange muted grandiosity of the events. I say muted because those who have perpetrated the act have included themselves in the annihilation it achieved (quite unlike, for instance, a recent American terrorist, who was only annihilated later, after we had the opportunity to take in the full pathetic sweep of his life's tantrum and its resulting "ideas," and also quite unlike those who merely recruit, train, and nurture the insecure with this or that religious "fundamentalism"—the Crusade, for instance, of these skyjackers). I say grandiosity because the annihilating moment, in this case, is so awe-full and fills our senses with such a keen appreciation of the massively destructive forces of reality (speed, steel, gravity), it is hard to retain the sense that it is a small group of men who are "doing" it. That is, that last and definitive moment seems to assert a cause that is bigger—more elemental—than any group of merely mortal men. This is similar to the climax of a Greek tragedy, wherein the tragic hero discovers that it was pure vanity on his part to think that he could have been the decider of his or of anyone else's fate. In that humbling moment, in the assertion of that inhuman (and indifferent) cause, we are distracted from our ordinary dream—that dream in which we feel we could possibly grasp the myriad causes of the myriad intentions that produce the myriad conditions of our lives.

My point here is really fairly simple. Indeed, its simplicity is what causes it to be so routinely overlooked. My point is this: in any tragedy, there is a victim (or victims) and there is a victimizer. It follows, then, that we have two opportunities: we could try to understand how the victim(s) felt, and/or we could try to understand how the victimizer(s) felt. If the victimizer is, as Greek tragedy suggests, always something bigger than—something more fundamental than—a mere man (i.e. Pride, Fury, Blindness To Mortal Fate, etc. . . .), then we *cannot* identify with it—we can only hope to learn about it and thereby learn to more gracefully submit ourselves to the basic conditions of existence that it implies. As for the victims, we have a somewhat easier time imagining how they must have experienced the terrible thing that compels their fame. We feel true pity for their misfortune, and true fear because their misfortune, in essence, is somehow bound to be ours. Put another way, we connect with the victims because they are, in essence and at bottom, what we are.

And this, I think, is where our "national reaction"

has gone sadly awry. I mean the flags and the patriotic songs and all that. Do we honestly imagine that "evil" and/or "madness" have produced more war than, say, "nationalism" and/or "religion?" A half-glance at any history book would dispel this notion decisively. But more to the point, if any one of us imagines him or herself on that plane, or in that stairwell, or anywhere in that tragedy—that is, if we sympathize with the actual victims in this incident—we cannot help but understand that the significant emotions that they felt *were not American emotions*. Not in the slightest. No, they were the emotions of our species. When falling out of the sky, when burning or choking to death, it is safe to say that a human being enters into a kind of experience that "nationality" cannot be relevant to. Indonesian or French passengers fall out of the sky with exactly the same sort of terrible fear as Americans do. Yes, this tragedy did occur in American air-space, with mostly American victims, and at decidedly American landmarks (symbols of American wealth and power), and so it is bound to concern Americans the most and bound to bring us closer together in our grief and our worry over the future we might be facing. One cannot help but feel, however, that the majority of the flag-waving is not concerned with "our" coming together as much as it is concerned with "our" distinguishing ourselves from "them," whoever "they" may turn out to be. This distinction between "us" and "them"—between American humans and humans from other countries—is a distinction that, at times, needs to be made. But not in this situation. In this case, and in any real tragedy, the distinction of nationality demonstrates a bizarre insistence on defining the victims in much more superficial terms than they deserve. Moreover, it is precisely this kind of sentiment (and the policy that this sentiment has developed) that has caused "us" to become a sadly isolated sort, the sort who feel, increasingly, entitled to be oblivious to the humanity of human beings who are not American.

Ask the average American to describe world affairs, or the impact of U.S. policy in world affairs, and you will see what I mean.

Such entitlement, if it is exercised with enough vigor, will no doubt produce enemies. It has. This brings us to the specific criminals in this case—criminals who, quite obviously, hated America (us?) *enough to give their own lives* for a chance to unleash a hellish spectacle upon it (and us). These men, the men who actually did this—actually boarded the planes and guided them to their destruction—these men are gone now. They were ash the moment they accomplished what they accomplished (and contrary to the inexplicable rhetoric of our president, their act *is* an act that will stand, insofar as any act will stand—ask the families of the victims if it stands). Likewise, the victims, the men and women who boarded the planes and were forcibly immersed in the horror I have (inadequately) described above, are gone—they were ash in the very same moment. And the story of their interaction with one another cannot now, for us, be made sense of, at least not in any way we can call satisfactory. The story that is sensible to us can barely be called a story; it's too short, too devoid of complication. Its significance does not come from the specific identities or nationalities of its victims; its significance comes from those who were *not* there. In a tragedy, it is always those who were not there who are left to conjure the meaning of the real story. And the real story, in this case, is that they rose up with confidence, when, in mid-air, something terrible happened, and they plunged, wordlessly, facelessly, into sure and complete obliteration. Yes, wordlessly, at least from our perspective. It's only us, in the afterwards, who have the words. Look at us. We sit with our words, day and night, and we try not to tell the story.

DEFINING GROUND ZERO

Lately, Lincoln's Gettysburg Address has gotten some attention from the rich people who read speeches on T.V. That's one of my favorite speeches—I actually have a hard time reading it without weeping sometimes. Some have said that it's impossible to make the Address fit our current "war" on terrorism. It is hard, I'd say, but not impossible, if we give it enough thought, and if we are willing and able to disengage from the shabby discourse that is now in place. Here are the last few sentences of the Address:

> But, in a larger sense, we can not dedicate—we can not consecrate—we can not hallow—this ground. The brave men, living and dead, who struggled here, have consecrated it, far above our poor power to add or detract. The world will little note, nor long remember what we say here, but it can never forget what they did here. It is for us the living, rather, to be dedicated here to the unfinished work which they who fought here have thus far so nobly advanced. It is rather for us to be here dedicated to the great task remaining before us—that from these honored dead we take increased devotion to that cause for which

they gave the last full measure of devotion—that we here highly resolve that these dead shall not have died in vain, that this nation, under God, shall have a new birth of freedom, and that government of the people, by the people, for the people, shall not perish from the earth.

Let me start with the notion of "freedom." President Bush uses this word a lot. He uses it as though it was the name of a lake or a mountain. There it is—Freedom—we have it, and because we have it, everything is nicer. Abraham Lincoln, on the other hand, was not a fool; he even wrote his own speeches. And Lincoln does not refer to freedom in the same way; he says, "a new birth of freedom," as though freedom was something difficult to achieve—as painful as it is joyous—and as though it was continually changing, becoming always more inclusive of people and of their chosen lives. His implication was that the end of American slavery was but *one* potential birth of freedom. His implication was that the struggle, "the unfinished work," to allow for the birth of new freedoms would not—could not—soon be finished. It would, so long as it truly stood for "the people," go on and on, and it would require, continually, the terrible sacrifice of those who are brave enough to fight for it.

In Lincoln's time, the earth was a radically different place; concepts of nationhood were different than they are now, and for good reasons. Lincoln's own pursuit of "nation" must be understood as not at all comparable to the nationalisms of our time. His main concern, we should note, is that a "government of the people, by the people, for the people, shall not perish from the earth." In this reference to the earth, it is implied that the kind of government he was fighting to maintain, and implicitly the kind of freedom its people might seek, was more than the destiny of one country. It was the destiny of all humankind, the destiny of "the people." If we read the address in this way—and I believe it is not foolish to do so—then the struggle, "the unfinished work," that lies before us is clearly defined, and it is global. Our task is not to embrace nationalism, which, while it proclaims itself a bringing together, is much more decisively a breaking apart. Our task is not to buy and to display flags that naïvely set us apart from the rest of the people on earth. Nor is it our task to demonize phenomena we have yet to understand. In this new age, our task, should we ever come to understand ourselves as "the people" Lincoln speaks of and for, is to commit ourselves to learning how we might become dignified citizens of "the earth," every inch of which is by now, surely, hallowed.

ABUNDANT HEALTH AND LEISURE

In 1680, a San Felipe Pueblo Indian named Pedro Naranjo was interrogated by the Spanish, who were attempting to determine how the Pueblo Rebellion of 1680 had been organized and executed. In that rebellion, over four hundred of the Spanish settlers were killed, and twenty-five hundred Spanish soldiers were driven south into Mexico. Naranjo described that the leader of the uprising, a shaman named Popé,

> "ordered in all the pueblos through which he passed that they instantly break up and burn the images of the holy Christ, the Virgin Mary and the other saints, the crosses, and everything pertaining to Christianity, and that they burn the temples, break up the bells, and separate from the wives whom God had given them in marriage and take those whom they desired. In order to take away their baptismal names, the water, and the holy oils, they were to plunge into the rivers and wash themselves with amole, which is a root native to the country, washing even their clothing, with the understanding that there would thus be taken from them the character of the holy sacraments . . ."

Naranjo went on to say that Popé:

> "had given them to understand that living thus in accordance with the law of their ancestors . . . they could erect their houses and enjoy abundant health and leisure."

MY HEART SAYS THERE'S NO PLACE TO GO

The President of the United States suggests that ecstasy is not good for you. He suggests you keep ecstasy out of your life. Lead a life without ecstasy. Surely you know who you are. Surely you know where you are. Surely you know what you are doing. Keep doing it. The President, with the unanimous support of the Congress, appreciates your efforts, and he is moved, really moved, by your confidence in who you are and what you are doing. Nobody does it better. Yes, it is true that you are headed into certain death. Let's face facts: your eyes, muscles, bones—someone you don't know will put them in the ground and they'll fall all apart. There will be nothing any longer to hold them together, and whatever it is that they held, whatever noble work they accomplished, they will cease to hold, cease to accomplish.

But do not let this keep you from your holiest of tasks! Go to work. Continue to watch the normally scheduled programming. Vote to build more prisons and give longer sentences to those who seek ecstasy. Vote to remove these monsters from the sacred free realm whereby you work and watch T.V. Hug your children. If you hug them tightly enough, they will carry on with your great work—they too will lead a life without ecstasy, and this will be your triumph, and the

United States of America, the greatest and the most civilized country in the history of the planet Earth, will thrive—will continue its drive toward an absolute certainty about its identity and its purpose.

Ecstasy will be sought by no one. Terror, in our time, may even be ended. Your grandchildren will be able to say: never again will terror or ecstasy be a part of this great country or of the many less civilized countries for which we so selflessly struggle.

But it will not be easy. There will be moments wherein you are tempted to seek ecstasy—moments wherein you drift, unsuspecting, toward ecstasy. Maybe you are in a luxury box somewhere—does it matter where?—and maybe there is free liquor. Maybe you begin to feel the crowd beneath you—the unluxurious crowd, from which you have been securely abstracted—and after a few drinks the crowd begins to sound to you like some wild animal caught in a trap—its beautiful agony and release from agony shimmering, shimmering—its beautiful agony and release from agony shimmering . . . and maybe, without intending to, you've been drinking too much, and you want now to continue to drink, you want to make yourself into a simple attentive hole—gloriously attentive— the kind of hole that this shimmering might really fill up. . . .

Do you see? Without intending to, you have sought out ecstasy. Luckily, and due to the greatness of American society, you are not in proximity to anything that will allow for this ecstasy to blossom—manifesting itself, for instance, as dance, or song, or—god forbid—an orgy.

Nonetheless, an ecstasy has developed, and this can lead very quickly to the downfall of the nation. You might say something foolish; you might fall and hit your head; you might even find yourself encouraging the wrong person to suck your dick—a person, that is, who is not legally sanctioned to do so. The risks of ecstasy may seem small, but remind yourself: this is the attitude that countless other countries have adopted, and look at what it has gotten them. Not the United States of America, I'll tell you that.

Before we had progressed to the fully human state we now enjoy, we used to dance. I don't mean that metaphorically. The land, back then, was a fire—we actually believed it was a fire. And we felt lucky to tend to it. Every day, this was the feeling: *lucky*. Sometimes it went out. Sometimes it roared up all around and consumed us. We danced in the ashes and we danced in the flames. We were ecstatic. Not always ecstatic, but consistently ecstatic, and as if that was what we were for. Imagine! Imagine living your life as though you were designed for ecstasy! Imagine a culture so perverse that it could assert that all persons should have easy access to ecstasy—that ecstasy is the expectable outcome of a person's existence!

To be fair, we must remember that we were not yet able, at that time, to imagine the mighty grandeur of computer programming, indoor plumbing, and all the magnificent structures they have afforded us. We were pathetic creatures, singing songs beneath the trees. I don't know that I can convey to you just how pathetic we were at that time. Perhaps the only way I can make you understand is to let you hear a song from back then. I hesitate to expose you—you who are free of ecstasy and desire for ecstasy—to the outpouring of such a crude psyche, but let it serve to remind you how far we have come. Here is the song:

> *I cry, I grieve, knowing we're to go away*
> *and leave these good flowers, these good songs.*
> *Let's be pleasured, let's sing. We're off to our destruction.*
> *Our friends are ill at ease? Sick, His hearts are vexed!*
> *We're not born twice, we're not engendered twice.*
> *Rather we must leave this earth.*
> *Near and in the presence of this company a moment!*
> *It can never be. I can never be pleasured, never be content.*

Where does my heart live? Where is my home?
Where does my mansion lie? True, I am poor on earth.
Poor as you are, my heart, don't grieve here on earth.
This seems to be my lot, and my heart knows it.
Where do I assign it? Is this my fate on earth?
It's known to be so. And so it's good, very much so.
My heart says there's no place to go.
What does God say? "We don't live, don't come here
    to stay, on earth."
I can't carry off these good flowers,
can't bring them down to the Place Unknown.
It's only for a moment.
We merely borrow these good ones, these songs.

DEC · 67 ·

SEMIOTICS: DEHISCENCE IS NEVER/ALWAYS SOUGHT

The disciples woke Jesus from a deep sleep and looked at him with a look of concern and worry that Jesus knew all too well. "You look concerned, or worried," said Jesus. "What is it?"

Thomas spoke up for the rest. "We have been hearing, or . . . well, we have reason to believe, or at any rate suspect . . ." He broke off, frustrated.

"Go on," said Jesus, "mere words cannot bring harm to the kingdom of heaven."

Judas picked up where Thomas left off: "You're a man, right?"

"I am a man and I am a son of man," said Jesus serenely.

"So you have a penis. . . ." said Judas.

Jesus did not look up. He looked down at his feet. "A man cannot be found in his body."

The disciples rolled their eyes, except for Peter, who, understanding where this was headed, pleaded with his Lord: "Jesus, we just want to know if you have a penis like the rest of us. It's not a spiritual question."

Jesus got up and began to walk away, but Thomas stepped in front of him. "Take off the robe."

Jesus sat down again and began to sob. Thomas put his hand on Jesus' shoulder. Jesus pulled violently away, squealing *"Get off!"* in a voice that no one had heard him use before. They were all quiet for a moment and then Jesus spoke again, calmer now, and with a new sort of resolve: *"I'll take it off."*

Standing up defiantly, he let the robe fall from his shoulders. What the disciples saw next shocked them. A few gasped. Jesus did not have a penis! In fact, he seemed to have a vagina. Mistrustful of appearances, Judas began to stammer toward the obvious pressing question: "Lord, you are . . . you have. . . ."

Jesus interrupted him belligerently: "I have a cunt— yes I do. I have a filthy cunt!"

"But . . ." said the disciples.

"Do you want to see it?" Jesus lay down on the ground and spread his legs. The apostles stared, wide-eyed, at their savior's vagina. "Peter, why don't you come down here and take a closer look? Come down here, all of you—have a good look! Peter, now! Down on your knees and lick your master's filthy cunt!"

Peter, to the surprise and the delight of the other disciples, approached the Lord and began to do as he was told.

"That's right—lick it good, lick that cunt—lick it 'til it's as clean as the mind of our holy Father."

Jesus rolled onto his side and maneuvered Peter into the 69 position. He pulled up Peter's robe and took his surprisingly small, fully erect cock into his mouth. "Thomas," Jesus shouted, "get behind me and fuck my ass while Peter licks my filthy cunt."

Thomas did as he was told. "This is heaven," said Jesus sweetly, "a dick in my ass, a dick in my mouth, and a tongue in my filthy cunt."

As the night wore on, all the disciples had their chance to lick the filthy cunt of their Lord—and most of them got blow-jobs, and got to fuck him, too. Jesus, though he was clearly in a lot of pleasure, never allowed too much of it to show. He moaned and he talked dirty, but he never lost control. All night, to his quivering body the disciples came and went . . . as they were told to do. In the morning, however, when Jesus was awakened by two dogs fighting in the street, he was utterly alone, and he reeked, as before, as always, with the sad wasted seed of Believers-In-The-Word.

MEMO: TO THE DEPARTMENT

It is my contention that every member of the Department has, at one time or another, fantasized about sucking a dick. I reckon that some have even done it. I don't think enough is made of this. It isn't that I find the situation troubling—*I do not* find the situation troubling. In fact, I derive a certain calm from it. That is the word that comes to mind—calm—when I think of someone, or everyone, sucking a dick.

You see . . . my generation, in America, grew up with pornography. We grew up looking at pictures of women—and in that rare special find, even pictures of men—sucking dicks. And there is a certain sort of dick-sucking picture—a certain genre, one might say—that has always interested me. It's the sort where the dick-sucker is looking right into the camera. It's a subspecies of portrait: *portrait with dick in mouth.*

I recall I had this prissy girlfriend one time . . . and we went over to visit a friend of hers, and this friend was a heroin-addict and had a heroin-addict roommate. Well, this roommate couldn't have been more than 19, and she had clearly lived a hard life; she dressed in the punk fashion and one did not get the impression that she was posing. But this one day she was dressed up more in the "trust me, I am mediocre" fashion—perhaps she had had to go to a job interview or something. And my prissy girlfriend says to her: "you look nice. . . ." To this the young woman replied: "you should see me with a dick in my mouth."

Her comment has always stayed with me. And I have come, finally, to wonder if everyone might look better with a dick in his or her mouth. Perhaps *better* isn't exactly the right word—perhaps nicer, or calmer, or more honest . . . I don't know. Think, for instance, of that little display case by the Department door—you know, the one with little dickless portraits of all the Department's members. If that case was filled with dick-sucking portraits instead, I think it would obviously be improved, and I think it would more faithfully convey exactly who is who.

But why is that? I've been thinking about it and what I've come up with is this: in truth, you always have a dick in your mouth. Whose dick is it? It's not an ordinary dick; it's the dick of the god that opened your mouth in the first place. And why did he open your mouth, and why does he hold it open with his dick? It is so that he may be pleasured! And so that he might come! And he does come—he comes in your mouth! One day you will choke to death from his coming! But until *that* very special day, you should be glad of the dick in your mouth. Be glad of its erratic issue. Be glad, too, that in truth you are not whole, and not discrete, and not in control of what comes into your mouth. And if you decide to have portraits taken, let those portraits distinguish you from the vain discretion at the heart of every devoted mediocrity.

THE LUMBERJACK'S MELANCHOLY PUSSY

I have for some time now been seeking to create for myself the sense that I am alive. It isn't easy. My effort, in fact, is almost exclusively humiliating, not only in terms of its amazingly complex history of failures, but also by way of the dismal barren camp it forces me to call home. There are not many of us, it seems, in "American life," and them that are not us do not find our plight respectable or amusing. Even so, I remain hopeful, and it is not my intention to waste any more of your precious time addressing my humiliation. Instead, I would like to turn yet again to the effort that so often defines me. I do so, as I said, primarily for myself, but let me in this one case—perhaps for my own satisfaction, perhaps not—assume that you are huddled nearby . . . and that you do not want me to shut up.

The drinking of alcohol has always been a favorite strategy of ours, and I'd like to pass along to you some thoughts on how to best pursue it. Many of us sit in bars or on couches and drink; rarely, though—oh so rarely!—does this result in a very strong sense that we are alive. This, I think, is because we tend *to talk* while we drink, and so long as we are mired in talk, the myriad assumptions that have deadened us remain healthy and active. What to do? In order that we feel alive, there need be something between us. Talk is one such something, but there are many other possibilities: music comes to mind, as does sport. Whatever we place between us, however, is faced with the same danger, and that is the danger of the thing coming to seem ordinary, the thing failing to jerk or float us up out of the zombie-progress we of necessity move around in.

I want to address *talk,* though, because I think there is a way—or there are ways—to feel alive via placing speech between us. Getting *very* drunk (putting both alcohol and talk at the same time between us) is one way to give talk a better chance, but in the long run this strategy proves brutal and produces ever-diminishing returns. Another way is to turn oneself into an audience that is subjected to a particular language-artist. I don't want to address that strategy here. I am proposing, here, something more casual, spontaneous, and democratic: the drinking game.

The drinking game seems to have gone out of style. Or is it that I have "outgrown" it—is it that I now inhabit the world of those who see the drinking game as an immature strategy? I don't know if the young still play drinking games the way we did, but I suspect they do. We played Quarters, Asshole, and other card games. I think I'd enjoy playing these still, though I fear I am no longer as capable of drinking at not-my-own-pace. I don't propose, here, that we older folks (I am at present 39) play any of these games; besides the amount-of-drink problem, there are the games themselves, which often allow for too much ordinary talk to erupt, and which generally fail to be interesting in and of themselves. I propose, rather, that we put in place new drinking games— drinking games more fitted to our place in life.

One such game I have invented. I have even gone as far as to play this game and I have thereby verified its goodness; it has produced again and again the sense that I am alive. The game is called *The Lumberjack's Melancholy Pussy.* Here is how to play. Assemble 4 to 8 persons. Sit at a table together, alcohols in hand. The oldest person at the table goes first and we proceed around the table clockwise. Each player, at his or her turn, must create a unique statement by choosing between certain words and filling in certain blanks within the following formula:

> I love/hate (choose one or the other) the lumberjack's (insert one word) (pussy/dick/asshole/cunt/balls/tits) because (insert a phrase to complete the sentence).

Here are some examples of what a player might create:

> *I love the lumberjack's doctor-sounding pussy because it keeps the lambs away.*

> *I hate the lumberjack's big dick because I was raised to hate what I cannot hear.*

> *I love the lumberjack's mellifluous tits because I am a kind of lobster.*

When a player has uttered his or her utterance, the other players, going clockwise, one by one—and quickly, quickly, for fuck's sake—give a thumbs up or a thumbs down. Thumbs up is a vote to accept the utterance as fitting and proper. One may define *fitting and proper,* of course, as one likes, though the gist, I suspect, is to validate what is surprising and/or in some way hints at or creates the sense of our being alive. Players, in casting their votes, should perhaps think of what Jesus says in the Gospel of Thomas: "If you bring forth what is within you, what you bring forth will save you. If you do not bring forth what is within you, what you do not bring forth will destroy you."

As for the actual drinking penalties, one can make adjustments to fit one's moods or potentials. I have usually played it so that more rejections than validations from one's peers means the player must take a drink. I recall once playing it another way wherein unanimous validation entitles the player to give a shot of bourbon to somebody, and wherein unanimous rejection meant the player must himself do the shot. While I myself feel affectionate toward instances of (and even the principle behind) forced drinking, many people in my current circles have come to feel otherwise, and so the game has usually not hinged on its forced-drinking aspect; rather, it has been simply a righteous context for casual drinking, which is to say, a way to keep ordinary talk from contaminating casual drinking.

So go ahead and try it. Go on. In my experience, it's been interesting to find out who's good at it and who's not so good—and then too who is so disturbed by it that he or she has to leave the room. There are people, it turns out, who are simply not up to it—people who cannot bear to situate themselves in the love/hate of words, which is really the love/hate of what the body is and wants. I've heard it said that I should feel sorry for those folks. Maybe that's so . . . but before I offer my sympathy I need first to see the way in which they walk out of the room. And it also depends on whether or not they go home and devote themselves to keeping me from playing.

I reckon there are really only two kinds of people in the world: those who are comfortable in the midst of The Lumberjack's Melancholy Pussy . . . and those who are not. I gather that the two groups have never lived together peacefully, and there seems to me no reason to think they ever will. It follows, then, that those of us who play must make it clear, in our laughter and in our drinking and in our choice of games, that we will not be intimidated—that we will not be made to cower or whisper quietly in dark corners. No, we will continue to pleasure ourselves, together, in the open; the open, after all, is as much our home as it is the home of those who live to have nothing between them.

IMPEDIMENTS TO DEMOCRACY

"Hey, Mr. Cocksucker...."

Mr. Cocksucker looked up from his USA Today. "Mr. Cuntlick. How does it go?"

Mr. Cuntlick sat down in the booth across from his friend. Mr. Cuntlick moved slowly, deliberately, as if he had a bad back. He stretched his arms over his head and spoke through a yawn: "Same old, same old. What's up with you? Sucking a lot of cock?"

"You know it. Sucked more cock this month than . . . well, let's see . . . the most since April of '97. You know how that month was."

Mr. Cuntlick nodded steadily. "April of '97 was a cocksucking month."

The two men sat quietly for a moment, not at all uneasy with one another.

Mr. Cuntlick continued: "How are they, though, these days—gettin' any big ones?"

Mr. Cocksucker folded his newspaper and sat it on the table, resigned to endure yet another definite quantity of talk. "Some. Had a guy just this morning must've been 10 inches if he was an inch."

"Can't argue with that."

"Yeah. How's things with you?"

"I can't complain. I do complain, I mean, but I shouldn't."

Mr. Cocksucker felt obligated to pursue the notion of his friend's well-being a step further: "Pussy's clean?"

Mr. Cuntlick sort of snorted a gentle and amused snort. "Never cleaner." There was nearly a significant pause before he continued: "It's kind of sad, though, you know, that you have to—well, that that's the question you have to ask. I'm not saying unclean pussy frightens me, though I guess it does, or it can. But I'm not saying that—I'm saying, for you there's the issue of size—how thick, how long. And what is there for me? Odor? Texture? It doesn't seem fair."

Mr. Cocksucker tried to soothe his friend: "Same level of pleasure, though, right? We all know that Tiresias story."

"On some level, maybe that's true. But in other ways, it's not true. Like talking about it. Talking about it is not nothing. . . . It's just not equitable . . . in terms of *drama*. A pussy is in every case just a pussy. Maybe you can say one pussy is hot or wet, or lippy or whatever . . . but my point is— it just doesn't hold a candle to *huge* . . . or *hung like a horse*. One cunt can't set itself apart from another cunt in the same way one cock can set itself apart from another cock—that's what I'm saying."

Mr. Cocksucker smiled: "Yeah, you're right. I mean you have a point. *Schlong* . . . "

"Exactly, schlong."

The waitress arrived at the table with a glass of water for Mr. Cuntlick. She looked at Mr. Cocksucker as she sat it on the table: "Can I get you another cup of coffee?"

"No thanks—just the check."

The waitress smiled and scurried off.

Mr. Cocksucker continued, offering an unnecessary explanation for his imminent departure: "Gotta get back to work."

Mr. Cuntlick seemed contented to have spoken his piece. Mr. Cocksucker sensed this and stretched his neck as he pulled a five dollar bill from his pocket and put it on the table. It was time to poke fun at his friend. "Why don't you come on with me? If cocks are so much better than cunts. . . . I mean . . . there's no shortage. You can have the first big one that comes in."

Mr. Cuntlick refused to smile: "I think I'd have to start small. Start too big right off and you got nothing to live for."

"My friend, if you're living for the schlong, you're not living at all. . . ."

"That's easy for you to say."

GENUINE PEOPLE: TALKING THIS WAY, EVERYTHING DISSOLVES

Robert Hass' poem, "Meditation At Lagunitas," is perhaps the most influential American poem of the past fifty years. That is to say, within the great quantity of "serious" poetry that has been written and published in that time, Hass' poem has had a great influence, and has come to stand for a kind of poem that is now understood to be possible, even worthwhile. "Meditation At Lagunitas" is the best example I have yet found of recent poetry's stand *against* poetic knowledge.

The poem opens with a joke about "all the new thinking." "All the new thinking is about loss./ In this it resembles all the old thinking." With this joke, the poet distances himself from "thinking"—his poem will not be a thinking, but will come forth instead as a "meditation," which we generally understand to be a kind of thinking that heals the world that knowledge has opened up, bringing the soul in meditation back into a oneness with where he is. The joke's being the very first act of the speaker should be noted. There is an immediate danger implied—the danger of thinking's possibly being new—but there is also an immediate extension of sympathy that is meant to conceal that danger, even to disprove it, and to create a *being one of us* that the audience is welcome to feel. If we are like the speaker and we feel some satisfaction in belittling the importance of recent theory (undoubtedly he is referring here to the emergence of *theory* into the American Academy)—then we have accepted his invitation and we have situated ourselves implicitly in the ranks of those who feel threatened by "theory." That "we" is set at ease, right from the start, knowing that *one of us* is speaking.

The speaker then moves on to offer a casual summation of the essential history of "thinking." As we know from the opening joke, thinking is all simply "about loss." Next, it is implied that thinking can be about loss in one of two ways: 1) "The idea, for example, that each particular erases/ the luminous clarity of a general idea." 2) "Or the other notion that . . . a word is elegy to what it signifies." These two examples of "thinking" "about loss" may seem ridiculously vague and incomplete, and we may wonder at the purpose of making such a statement. How could such a statement be poetic, or advance poetic insight? We need to recall the way that the joke has functioned; it has established that the poem's true audience is a we that does not value "thinking," new or old. For this audience, "the idea" and "the notion" do not appear vague or incomplete; they are not understood as cliché because "we" do not desire thinking's development—"we" have already defined ourselves as those souls who do not want to go the way of "theory." This we understands, moreover, that the speaker could not possibly develop "thinking" *because he is a poet*—he is already in the encounter that the poem is, and such an encounter distinguishes his substance from the substance that could desire to seek "theory." The difference between the poet and the theorist is not circumstantial—it is implied here as substantial. The substance of the speaker (and the substance of the we that his speech safeguards) is a substance essentially different from the substance that makes up the theorist; it is different, above all, in that it is not given to dissolution.

Clearly, this speaker speaks from and for the genuine realm. He makes philosophical-sounding statements only to bankrupt them by hinting at his privileged grasp of scenic ground. The radiance of his scenic ground lies in its specificity, its being given to him in such a way that his speech makes it radiant. "The clown-/ faced woodpecker, probing the dead sculpted trunk/ of that black birch." How, we might ask, is the woodpecker's being *clown-faced,* or the tree's being a *black birch,* significant to the poem? If we insert "red-headed" for clown-faced, or "oak" for black birch, does the meaning of the poem change? Absolutely not. The high level of specificity serves here, and in the rest of the poem, only to create the glorious power of the poet, which is his ability to register, and thereby *keep,* the scene. The various scenes in the poem shine with the goodness of those who hold them humbly in their possession. "Blackberry," in the poem, shines *so* dramatically that it warrants italics. The difference between the poem and an explicitly sentimental ad for something that celebrates one's casual comfortable life . . . is slight; "loss" is more apparent in the poem—it is explicitly named. Subsequently, the poem struggles more self-consciously to arrive at the "numinous" moment that an ad can immediately glory in.

Line twelve at last breaks off from the speaker's effort to establish thinking's bankruptcy and begins to move toward revealing his privileged encounter with what is. The "we" that "talked about" loss turns out, of course, to be a specific we—the speaker and his friend—but it is also the we that the audience can feel itself to be, the we who has just now been immersed in the speaker's talk of "loss." Each we arrives at the same point, experiencing "loss" as a "thin wire of grief, a tone/ almost querulous." Each we, with the help of the speaker, turns away from the disruption that this "thin wire of grief" threatens to allow for. The speaker experiences the arising of obscenery as a "thin wire," which is to say, as a ground that one cannot possibly come to stand upon, and a ground that one would not even benefit from standing upon (one would be there merely to *whine?*). How different this conception is from Faulkner: "Before us the thick dark current runs. It talks up to us in a murmur become ceaseless and myriad, the yellow surface dimpled monstrously into fading swirls traveling along the surface for an instant, silent, impermanent and profoundly significant, as though just beneath the surface something huge and alive waked for a moment of lazy alertness out of and into light slumber again." Not a "thin wire," but a "thick dark current" "runs" "before us." "Before," in the Faulkner passage, means both "prior to" and "lying in front of;" with this one word, then, Faulkner immerses his speaker in the poetic ground—it is, like the slumber it continually disturbs, impossible for him to be apart from that ground.

Hass' speaker could not be situated more differently; poetic ground is, for him, *naturally uninhabitable,* a small "grief" that makes itself apparent in the "thin wire" of "the voice" that one cannot make a stand upon. The speaker goes on to say, "After awhile I understood that,/ talking this way, everything dissolves." Here is the first revelation of the speaker's privileged grasp of scenic ground. When he says that "everything dissolves," he means that, in "thinking," or in a poetry that is the careful articulation of the coming of a scene that can't be kept, there is ultimately nothing meaningful—that *all* meaning, *all* being, is simply dissolved by such a poetry. "Thinking" "about loss," then, for those of us who always already grasp the world in its truly radiant specificity, is a simple waste of time; thinking might even be implied as an irresponsibility, a failure to celebrate our good essence, our being the good keepers of the genuine realm.

By listing particular irreducible elements of the genuine realm, the speaker demonstrates the real impossibility of articulating the coming of a scene that can't be kept. "Talking this way, everything dissolves: *justice,/ pine, hair, woman, you* and *I.*" If we set aside, for the moment, "pine" and "hair," we are left with "justice," "woman," "you" and "I." That is, we are left with just two lovers, *you and I,* and the mystical condition of the realm that sustains them: justice. "Pine" and "hair" are added to the list to bring across (again) the speaker's miraculously concrete grasp of the scene; "pine" and "hair" radiate their concreteness out into the more abstract you, I, and justice . . . and in this way we are encouraged to feel the full depth and breadth of the genuine realm.

We have moved now, with this list, into a confession of the privilege that has been implied all along. This privilege is somewhat complicated by the conspicuous presence of "loss," which "thinking" cannot encounter, but which the speaker of the poem can and must encounter, somehow. . . . What remains to be revealed is just this somehow—the speaker's own specific encounter with loss, and how this encounter can know of loss *without thinking it,* without understanding it as the necessary ground of the present. That is, how can a speaker who is at home in the genuine realm, in the keeping of scenic ground, really know the coming of a scene that can't be kept . . . and still remain himself?

After the list, the speaker moves right into his own specific loss. He has clearly demonstrated that the ground of the present, the ground from which and for which he speaks, is not loss; he has to turn to his past, then, to find loss. He remembers two scenes, a woman he made love to, and the "muddy places" of his childhood river. Both are lost . . . in that they are past. And yet, as we hear of these scenes, what is striking is the speaker's "violent wonder," which holds these scenes up for the reader as powerfully satisfactory memories. This "violent wonder" is clearly representative of the speaker's essence; he is the powerful keeper (the seer and the remembrance) of the scenic ground. He is the lyrical camera moving over the shining mute bodies of the genuine realm, present and past. There lurks, beneath the present, a lost past, and with the emergence of this lost past, the speaker is faced with the challenge of how to keep the inevitability of loss from hollowing out his present.

He finds that the answer to his dilemma lies in the direction of his ability to *marvel* at how definitively he once possessed the lost scenes. He comes, that is, to wonder at what it is that allowed him to possess those scenes, once, so powerfully. And his answer is simple: it is the arising of his own essence (and, if the poem is working, of *our* essences), which is *genuine people*. He is the powerful keeper of the scenic ground, and the arising of his own sense of himself makes specific loss irrelevant. How so? The arising of his essence establishes one thing above all else, and that is that *the good*, the very substance of the genuine, will forever continue in us, even if the specific manifestations it arrives at cannot remain. "It hardly had to do with *her*," (my italics) the speaker says.

The speaker, dedicated to the celebration of his own power, his endless keeping of scenic ground, is yet resigned to dwell in the gentle sadness, the "longing," that he understands must be built in to this State. Why, he wonders, is longing built into his essence? And his answer: "because desire is full of endless distances." These "endless distances" are the very fabric of scenic ground's persistence; the genuine person does not experience the possessed scenes of his own past as lost; instead, they are simply concealed in a distance, into which he is then forever bound to "long." It is "long" from scene to scene to scene, but they *do* cohere—and he *is* their coherence. The speaker's own specific losses have led him to define the way in which it is possible for him to experience loss; he does not "think" about, dwell on, or give himself over to the coming of a scene that can't be kept; instead, he resigns himself to "longing." He resigns himself to casually re-inhabiting the still-intact scenes that recede into the mystical origin of his wholeness. By using "we say" in his definition of "longing," the speaker invokes (again) the we-centered power of the genuine realm, the power that stems from being truly *one of us*. "I must have been the same to her" works in much the same way, asserting that longing is not just my state—it is the essential state of all true or genuine persons—the state of every person blessed with a chasmless residence in the genuine realm.

"I must have been the same to her" is also a kind of turning away from the poem itself and into the past; it is a pause, by which a new kind of engagement with things is called for. Here, in this pause, the speaker turns back into longing and comes out of it even more convinced of his essence as the true possessor of scenic ground. "But I remember so much." The "so much" is the real step here; with this "so much" the speaker performs *such* a powerful possessing of the "lost" scene that he radically disengages himself from understanding it as lost. Immediately after the "so much," he formulates himself as precisely this mystical disengagement: "There are moments when the body is as numinous/ as words, days that are the good flesh continuing." This is the statement from which all of the poem's other statements have originated. The speaker asserts, here, that there does indeed exist a State in which scenic ground is possessed; there is indeed a space in which bodies are genuine and "continue" in the "good" of genuine flesh.

The unfamiliarity of the word "numinous" might distract us, and it seems to function above all to conceal the statement's egregious vanity, but we can take this word as a conspicuous description of that glow that marks the whole of the poem and makes it equivalent with an explicitly sentimental ad for that which allows us our casual comfortable lives. "Numinous" means "attended or kept by a divinity." This is exactly the state of bodies in the genuine realm—they glow with the happiness of being secure in their mystical createdness, of being maintained by a higher power, forever "continuing" under its care. The bodies do not need to be spoken into identity, for they are already there—they need not words . . . for they are already, in their very substance, given to us in a specific and fully satisfactory way. They are "the good flesh" of "days" gone by, but gone by in such a way that they have revealed to us who we remain. "The good flesh" rather explicitly names the substance of the possessors of the scenic ground. This poem may be described as an invocation of this substance, which, where it is successful, brings solace to the specific possessors it makes up, the apparently unified subjects trapped in the sigh—the slight discomfort—of longing.

The good flesh, as it arises to celebrate itself and to resign itself to the endless distances of longing, conceives of itself as based in a "tenderness." That is, the good flesh tends to the specificity of the world that is always already given to it, and it basks in the magical length of this tending's success; in turn, it feels tended to by the mystical creator of its given realm. The poem closes, fittingly, with a child's insistence on a naïve sense of the power of language, a sense which arises to secure the implicit eternity of the genuine State. Childish eternity is at the heart of the genuine State—it is what the speaker most needed to protect from "loss." He has done so by looking back into the radiance of his own possessed scenic grounds, the most magical of which lies in his own privileged childhood (and this poem, in my view, could not have been written by a nonwhite American), which is the first arising of his genuine essence, his being the blessed owner of the scenic ground. The poem re-establishes the "tenderness" of childish eternity for the speaker and for the we who shares in his substance, his "good" flesh.

By closing in this fashion, the poem leaves its audience to linger in the joy of that re-establishment, even if each audience-member is no longer a child, and so must now simultaneously endure the "thin wire of grief" that longing necessitates. The we of the genuine realm is situated in just this way, lodged between the joy of its childish essence and the mild pain that cannot disrupt this essence; indeed, the poem's primary function is to demonstrate that this disruption cannot take place—cannot undermine the genuine State. So situated, the speaker stands against "thinking," which too steadily inhabits the pain of loss. He also stands, in the irreducibly moral stance of every soul engendered by the genuine State, in recognition of his responsibility to celebrate his dominance as his good essence and his blessed ownership of genuine scenes.

Meditation At Cleveland

All the new thinking is about drugs.
In this it resembles all the old thinking.
The idea, for example, that each bong-hit erases
the tedious progress of industrial society. That the clown-
faced hippie stocking the Snack and Treat shelves
of this massive new Wal-Mart is, by his presence,
some tragic bellying forth of a final sleep
full of the unapologetically polite. Or the other notion that,
because there is in this world no one thing
to which the murmur of *dilaudid* corresponds,
a drug's name is powerless babysitter to what it signifies.
We talked about it late last night and in the voice
of my friend there was a thin wire of confusion, a slur
almost querulous. After awhile I understood that,
popping pain-killers this way, everything dissolves: *puppy,
poopy, pussy, peenie, hair, you,* and *I.* There was a man
I made love to and I couldn't remember how, having
no recollection of meeting him or bringing him home. Still,
I felt a violent wonder at his huge penis
like a thirst for water after drinking whiskey and eating
a whole bag of pork rinds, the spicy kind we called
*bah-bee-*Q. It hardly had to do with his penis.

Schlong, we say, because dick is too familiar
to describe such length. I must have blacked out.
But now I remember so much, the way he pulled handfuls
      of hair
out of my head, the thing his dad said that hurt him, what
he stole from my house. There are moments when a huge penis
is as numinous as words, nights that are the good flesh
      parting.
So high, those afternoons and evenings,
saying *schlong, schlong, schlong.*

AN EYE FOR AN EYE FOR AN EYE

This Queer Eye idea has real potential. I would like to see it pursued more seriously. For instance, why not have a *Queer Eye for the Queer Eye for the Straight Guy?* It could air right after *Queer Eye for the Straight Guy.* It would consist of five gay guys who have just watched *Queer Eye for the Straight Guy,* and these guys would analyze, in depth and with attitude, the appearance and the pronouncements of the Fab 5. I love to watch *Queer Eye . . .* but the more I watch, the more I feel, as a straight guy, that I am incapable of the proper withering critique of the Fab 5 itself. And the more I ask myself: can these five Queers be *the* Queer Eye? Certainly not. There are many Queer Eyes in the world, and many of these would, no doubt, be able to take the Fab 5 to task, allowing viewers—well, straight viewers anyway—a better sense of the whole phenomenon. As it stands, the Fab 5 are the Fab 5 because they are immune to critique. It's as if they are truly the authorities on how to live, and as if this authority stems from some monolithic essence of Queerness. To dispute their authority would enrich the debate over what Queerness is . . . and would make the whole "advice" process much more profound.

One might take another approach; *Straight Eye for*

the Queer Eye for the Straight Guy. Here, understanding would cease to be the focus. Five straight guys, unable to understand or provide a pithy critique of the Fab 5, would instead focus on what the *Queer Eye's* "advice" fails to grasp. The program would work to restore complexity to the whole project by counterbalancing the *Queer Eye's* wisdoms with the Straight Guy's irreducible "tastes," many of which are as valid as the tastes implicit in Queer wisdom. Without this counterbalance, the show risks making the foolish assumption that the Straight Guy has no tastes at all—that he is a blank slate, so to speak, and can be simply filled in, decorated, and routed. No, the Straight Guy will retain, no matter what his makeover puts in place, certain Unqueer impulses or preferences, and, if the makeover is going to have any real chance of effecting significant change, these impulses or preferences should be acknowledged and to some extent catered to.

But the basic idea—the basic structure of the show—need not restrict itself to sexual preference. Why not: *Drug-users' Eye for the Corporate Zombie?* In this show, five drug-users (let's say, a heroin addict, a crack addict, an alcoholic smoker, a pain-killer addict, and a marijuana and sometime peyote user) could get together at the house or apartment of some Corporate Zombie . . . and completely remake his view of the world. This show could not be like *Queer Eye* in terms of episodic development. That is, each "case" would take more than a few days, and would need more than just one one-hour-long episode; the Drug-using Fab 5, because of the nature of their insight, would need months to get the job done. Over these months we would see the Corporate Zombie changing before our very eyes. But which drug will be right for him? There's plenty of lively debate on that point, you can be sure! I would program my Tivo so that I'd miss not one episode.

Another possibility is: *Rich Eye for the Poor Guy.* In this show—a show, by the way, that would be quite similar to many episodes of *Queer Eye for the Straight Guy*—five wealthy guys would descend upon some ghetto apartment or some trailer-park hovel and proceed (after installing a top-flight security system, of course) to transform the interior so that it resonates with a solidly upper-middle-class atmosphere. The "culture" expert would explain how to appear as though the school in one's neighborhood had been very well-funded, and would introduce the poor guy to the sort of music those with a decent job (with benefits) would listen to. Also, practical tips would be shared: how one should NEVER ride public transportation, for instance. If need be, this show could be framed a bit differently, if its producers sought a broader appeal: *American Eye for the Third World Guy*. Same concept.

Or how about: *Dying Eye for the Healthy Guy?* Five terminally ill guys descend upon the abode of a Healthy Guy, and they bring with them a unique sense of how a Healthy life might best be pursued. This show may turn out to be quite akin to *Drug-Users' Eye for the Corporate Zombie*. But maybe not. The only way to know for sure is to get going and make the shows. I only hope we're up to it. It is scary to think of how much great advice dies in the womb.

WITHSTANDING SEIZURE

Seizure

To me he seems like a god
as he sits facing you and
hears you near as you speak
softly and laugh

in a sweet echo that jolts
the heart in my ribs. For now
as I look at you my voice
is empty and

can say nothing as my tongue
cracks and slender fire is quick
under my skin. My eyes are dead
to light, my ears

pound, and sweat pours over me.
I convulse, greener than grass,
and feel my mind slip as I
go close to death,

yet, being poor, must suffer
everything.

—

It is not easy to stand with a world as convulsive as
this one. It is difficult. This world, in truth, is a sea—it heaves
and bursts and pulls itself apart. And we are not above this
world except in pretend. It is not easy to stand here, *as* here—
and yet it is perhaps just as difficult *not* to stand here. That is,
even if our whole goal is to stand apart from the convulsive
world, and even as we seek with all our might to establish
ourselves upon an other firmer ground, this sea comes over
us. Of course there are "success" stories—there are those
who seem to stand, for a time, upon an other firmer ground.
While it is true that this firmer ground is manifest materially
(and so, is always dependent upon the maintenance of
discreet financial and social systems), it is always first and
foremost an imaginary ground. For this imaginary ground
to be maintained, one must keep in place a specific kind of
imaginary practice.

This kind of imaginary practice might be described
as a safeguarding of the self against poetic knowledge. The
development of such a practice seems inevitable, and hardly
monstrous, so long as it remains humble enough to confess,
consistently, its significant failure. That is, the instinct to
connect with the world as it truly stands, convulsing, is as
inevitable, or as pressing, as the instinct to maintain for
oneself a firm ground. For me, the struggle to reconcile
and accommodate these seemingly contradictory instincts
is the fundamental struggle beings face; it is the struggle to
evolve the imagination of a firm ground that is not rigid, not
naïve—a firm ground that is not set against, and that can
withstand, the convulsions that make it live and die, appear
and disappear.

Poetic speech is clearly unique in its power to manifest

such a ground—a ground which, while it is in some sense firm, nevertheless understands its stability as but a necessary delusion. In poetic speech, the firmness of imaginary ground is a firmness already subtly possessed of the convulsion(s) of the real (the unimaginable); the horizon that poetic speech conjures up nurtures that border, that inherently compromised space wherein it is impossible to see exactly where oblivion begins and order ends. Indeed, if the poet is to be reckoned as powerful, it is because of this possession—because she has found a way of capturing (resonating with) the force of the impending unimaginable, and in such a way that the imaginary ground—the speaker herself—is implied as a corresponding power, at least to the extent that she is able to withstand, even capture, the convulsion that informs and sustains the limits of her ownmost project. The poet is powerful, in short, because she is able to thrive in the shadow of that horizon, that border, and is able to know that it will cross over her just as she crosses over it.

Sappho's poem, "Seizure," makes us think more carefully about the way in which the poet's experience is convulsive. To "convulse" is to show evidence of inward disruption; it is to be penetrated by something that one cannot abide . . . but at the same time cannot reject. When one convulses, one's imagined unity is shaken and made awkwardly apparent . . . but it is not dissolved; one remains in some sense together, as one body/self, even as that body/self trembles with the secret disruption that has caused it to lose its ordinary power, which was the power to remain firmly upon its way. There is a phrase that I have seen in Homer that is generally translated: *loosens his limbs*. It is used to describe death in battle; when a warrior is speared, for instance, it is said that he has had his limbs loosed. The phrase speaks to the moment of losing one's power, one's grasp; the warrior is still conscious in this terrible moment, but his power, his hold on fate, has been disrupted. I thought it was curious, then, when I saw the same phrase in Sappho's poem, "To Atthis":

Love—bittersweet, irrepressible—
loosens my limbs and I tremble.

Here, the convulsion caused by "love" is compared with the moment wherein a warrior is felled by a mortal blow. What are we to make of this comparison? Is this analogy simply a sentimental exaggeration? Clearly, the blow that love delivers is not the blow that war delivers. What is to stop us from hearing this as a weak analogy? For Sappho, the focus is not the blow, but the convulsion that the blow causes—the seizure, the trembling, in the blow's wake. Love's "weapon" is never specified; the analogy never extends in that direction. The poet's encounter with "love" has caused her to be filled up with something that she cannot abide, yet cannot reject, and here is where the analogy transcends its seeming sentimentality. Rather than being a trite exaggeration of emotional distress, the analogy is a subtly executed glimpse of the physical/mental convulsion that is at once the foundation and the destiny (the end and the beginning) of imagination. This glimpse implies that we continually, "irrepressibly," suffer blows to our grasp of where we are, and so, continually lose control of our way through the world. Just as a felled warrior, in his final moment, looks out across a chasm at the scene he has suddenly been divorced from, so too a lover gazes, struck by the voice or the face of the one she loves and cannot possess, reeling before the chasm that holds the two apart.

In every blow, one kind of imagination practice (the kind that allows the subject to stand securely apart from the convulsions of the real) is disabled, and another kind of imagination practice is forced to arise. We might call the former: *imagination asleep and dreaming,* and the latter:

imagination waking. Imagination, asleep, does not cease to be imagination—no, it continues to function, dreaming, creating scenes. It is only different from imagination waking in that the scenes it creates are not withstanding (not standing with) reality's complexity. Imagination, faced with waking, is faced with the same project that imagination asleep is faced with: create a scene. And yet, imagination awaking must do so without the power to overlook reality, which is to say, without the power to overlook the fundamental instability of its images. This instability may seem, at first, to be merely a nullifying force—blurring and hollowing out the scene—and yet it becomes, ultimately, if the poet succeeds, the birthing of a new grasp of images, a new scene. This new grasp, because it resonates with a proximity to the annihilation it has just overcome (and which has promised to always return), invests the on-going clarity of the imagined scene with the full strangeness of its being-there. The speaker, in a poem, takes a stand in this chasm, a chasm which is simultaneously a deathbed and birthing place; she takes a stand in the yawning chasm between the real and the imaginary, and, by believing in the real, brings closure to where she has been, thus creating the need for a whole new being-there.

Sappho's poems have impacted upon my own practice of writing in a unique way. Her work, more than any other, has taught me that the poem is always an act of love, or at least always begins by implying an act of love, and stemming from it, resisting it, or lamenting it. The poet is inevitably a lover, but not a simple lover, not a lover who is able to trust in the love-project. While she loves, she at the same time knows the limit of love, the fate of every lover; this is what makes her love poetic. While poetic speech may create a powerful sense of the speaker's yearning to possess a specific scene (and within the scene, the possession of a specific other), it only does so because the poetic speaker stands in a uniquely impotent relation to the loved scene. Instead of residing in the power to make her way through the world, the poet's power is shifted toward the power to stand in, to stand *with,* the real world, which no longer offers a through. Both of these powers, of course, are short-lived, and unable to come into their fullness; these powers, that is, erode one another constantly.

In the poem "Seizure," I am not as much interested in the specific social contexts of the speaker's desire as much as I am interested in what said contexts arrive at, the description of the convulsion itself: "I convulse, greener than grass." To me, these two lines are some of the most potent lines of poetry I have ever encountered. The metaphor is simple and direct, yet resonates with two inextricably bound complexities—the complexity of an I (the imaginary) and of Nature (the real). Underlying the metaphor is this basic equation: *I am grass.* The I, like grass, is unshakeably passive, and utterly vulnerable to the conditions of its existence, which is to say, its being penetrated by what sustains (and ultimately destroys) it. Such passivity is at the heart of the poet's own seizure. The love that the speaker is swept up into must be at first assumed as her own definitive potential, her own inclination, and yet that potential, by going unfulfilled, transforms her—it reverses the field and makes *her* the beloved, the penetrated. She is penetrated, moreover, not by an other; she is penetrated the way that grass is penetrated by sunlight; she is penetrated by *knowledge of the whole of the scene* in which she imagines herself to dwell. She becomes, via this knowledge, receptive to everything there is or can be.

This transformation is as joyful as it is painful, and Sappho's metaphor is uniquely able to convey this. The I, in its convulsion, is not *as green as* grass—it is *greener* than grass. This means that the I's convulsion, when it is brought into imagery, is *more real* than the real. This is so for two reasons: a) because the real (the unimaginable) is only ever suspected *as real* in the moment of the poet's becoming conscious of her own impotence, her own inability to bring reality to specificity; and b) because the I, which had understood itself as the imaginary's natural sovereign, is suddenly subservient to unspeakable forces, which, when they are known of, call into question imagination's guiding intention.

In poetic space, images attain their greatest radiance, and yet they do so only because that which holds them is understood as a non-unified non-eternal field. The speaker of poetic speech is a field of grass in bright sunlight; the light is fire, and the grass, if it had not developed a receptive stance, would be consumed by this fire. The grass, in the fire, no doubt comes "close to death," and yet, is able to survive, and even to flourish. Certainly it is possible to argue that Sappho's closing lines depart altogether from the grass metaphor, returning most importantly to her social "poverty" as a woman in the realm of patriarchy. And yet, even this specific poverty must radiate now with a more fundamental poverty. The "everything" that the speaker "suffers" is the suffering not of any one thing . . . but of everything, which is to say, the condition of the imagination. Thus, suffering "womanhood" and suffering "existence" blur into the trajectory of one condition, one painful/joyful being in love.

It is important to recognize that "suffering," here, can be understood in two ways. First, it is the convulsion itself, the I's moment of being burned, penetrated, and thus, "greener than grass." Second, and more profoundly I think, it is the moment wherein the burning *ceases*, the moment wherein death *withdraws* and the speaker sinks back into a non-convulsive state. In this latter reading (which reminds one of certain Dickinson poems that end with a death that seems co-extensive with a return to the rut of everydayness), the "everything" that is suffered is history itself, the very process of recognizing and enduring love's inevitable failures. In this reading, it is interesting that the source of mortal suffering is not *death*—quite to the contrary. That is, the I's poverty is not its being bound to die—but rather, its being bound to love, its being incapable of being timeless, its being incapable of pursuing the radiance of the world into its full or endless manifestation. The mortal's mortality, that is, consists not of her being towards death, but of her being bound *into* time, her being bound into the *next* love just as much as into the dimmed radiance of loves lost.

⸺

Ex-Lover Somewhere

now to me you are a flower
alive backwards
            moving from bloom
to seed
  in high speed
slow motion
(we have seen this in school)
retracting beauty—
discernible shape, color—
with tremendous patience,
every delicate feature taken back
inside
the silent film

⸺

My own poem, "Ex-Lover Somewhere," is founded in one image—that of a flower on a film that is being run backwards. It seems to me that this image conveys several things concerning the practice of love. First, and most obviously, it recognizes a decay, a once-real beloved becoming mere image, image stored on film. And yet, the once-real beloved is acknowledged as being "Somewhere," being still real, and so, being in some sense immune to this process of decay. Because of this acknowledgement, the "living backwards" takes on more significance; the image of the beloved is not simply decaying, or perhaps is not decaying at all; she is not dying but is living in a different direction. The lost beloved, "living" in the speaker's "mind," has become or is moving toward becoming fully imaginary; as such she may represent a decaying specificity, but she might just as properly be understood as the birthing of an ambiguity, a "seed."

This birthing, however, like the film itself, is backwards—the distinct "features" that defined the beloved are not brought out into the light but are instead "taken back inside," where they assume a new power, the power of the anonymous, which is the power of the unspeakable. The film itself can be felt, here, as a devouring, as the silence into which all speech, all distinction, is made to turn. As the poem turns into this silence, an anonymous lover, the poet himself, is felt, and he is an endurance of his own practice of love; he is that which has not been worn away by love's continual failure. Sappho's poems have taught me many things, but above all they have helped me to understand that poems must be simultaneously simple and difficult. They are simple insofar as they must at least begin from an act of love, establishing the poet as a lover of where he has been. They are difficult insofar as they must then proceed to withstand, even joy in, the seizure that, while it divorces lover from beloved, nevertheless secures a new birth of love, a new grasp of the "everything" that might be suffered.

OUTSIDE THE HOSPITAL

Insofar as a good-bye is uttered truly, it marks a new relation to what is. So that the speaker of good-bye can embrace the newness of this relation, language empties itself of its statement-oriented meaning. For most of us, the specific events that obviously call for this embrace are somewhat few and far between, even if they're inevitable. This is where poetic speech comes in; once there has been the attempt to say good-bye, there is a new kind of knowledge; one has come to know, via this attempt, that saying good-bye is necessary. Poems come from the lingering and unembraced knowledge that past attempts to say good-bye have opened up; they are an attempt to reconcile ourselves to being upon the way to no where, to expose ourselves to the incomparable sense lying in that way. Knowledge of the other's being impossible to keep leads to a deeper insight: one's own self is impossible to keep. One's own self, taken as an already-there entity, is as bound into the forever shattering ground of language as anything it claims to possess. Derrida: "No one remains, *a priori.*" I think poetic speech, then, is well defined as the practice of saying good-bye to one's self.

This became more apparent to me recently when I was asked to write about where one of my poems came from.

In looking at the specific poem, I became aware of my own tendency to want to repair stories. So many of the stories I hear are completely out of touch with our real situation— they are, in fact, designed to further the idea that reality can be "successfully" transcended. Capitalist culture generates many such success stories, even as it obsesses on the bizarre traumas that might undermine them. Poetic speech, too, can be understood as such an undermining, but its undermining is different in that it goes further and insists that a discovery of some kind arise from this event. The discovery is always the same, in essence: the situation we are in, in truth . . . will not be transcended. Such a discovery, I believe, is important.

———

Outside The Hospital

He says
when they made this place
they sure knew what they were doing.
He carries the dead woman
every day from her grave
in the shining sky down
into a small garden,
where a light snow is falling.
He is her lover, and he brings her here,
knowing he is not allowed to bring her here.
She sees the flowers he's planted
and thanks him,
and tells him what their names are.
He says he will never forget them.
They're lying on the ground
beside snow-dusted flowers.
She's in love with the ground
and the flowers,
but not with their names,

and not with him, who is saying them.
She hears him, feels his face
next to her face.
She wants to be in love.
Disappearing forever is the only solution.

—

"Outside The Hospital" comes from a soap-opera story-line, the story of Scotty and Dominique on *General Hospital*. I watched the story and found that the transcendence it struggled to assert was completely absurd—so deeply unbelievable that I was fascinated by it. Here is, briefly, the story. Scotty and Dominique fall in love; they are both *completely* happy, and their happiness rests completely in their having, in their fully knowing, one another; Dominique is then diagnosed with terminal brain cancer; eventually she dies in Scotty's arms, and he finds the strength to go on only because one of her eggs has been artificially inseminated and placed in the womb of the couple's best friend, Lucy.

This story is a version of the movie "Dark Victory," but it has been changed—it has been made less dark by the introduction of the fetus, which in some small but decisive way claims to be a successful maintenance of the beloved, the already-there entity that was known as Dominique. This claim enables the postponement of a full good-bye. The unthinkable loss, the loss of the whole foundation of the world, is gotten around. I was interested in this change of story—not the specific change, but the fact that a change, a less "dark" view, was necessary. It seemed to me that this postponement of complete grief was conspicuously ordinary, and conspicuously unconvincing. In re-storing the story, then, I re-tell it from the position of the beloved, the position of the one who, like every real one of us, is having to die a real death.

Sometimes the sheer simplicity of our pain is beauti-ful. *I love you—you are everything—and now . . . I must lose you forever.* Melodrama often provides access to such pain, even when it makes an effort and takes absurd mystical turns to re-conceal it. This is why I watch soap operas. The most important story-line, for me, is that of the lover's eternally successful maintenance of the beloved, which might also be called: *discovering the impossibility of real loss.* The beloved, in this story-line, stands for the very potential of a world to be specific, to be known, and then he or she is in some way lost. The lover struggles against the loss of either the beloved's body (car wrecks into ocean, and no body is found, or the beloved dies, but there is a ghost . . .), or the beloved's specific identity (amnesia sets in, or the beloved is forced by a villain to keep his identity a secret). The one constant in the story is that the lover always arrives back at a happy re-discovery of the beloved, who was never *really* lost. In the story of Scotty and Dominique, what was odd was how Dominique was, even for a soap opera, unsaveable.

The story found a way to get around embracing complete grief—found a way around *needing* poetic speech—but its viewers still had to feel, rather keenly, the unthinkability of the loss. This unthinkable loss lurks just beyond, and indeed saturates, the absurd postponement that the creation of the fetus means to enact. Two lovers stand looking at one another, having claimed that each to the other is the foundation of the knowability of the world. But one is already dead, or at the very least her mortality has been made too conspicuous, so the whole project of an other is hollowed out, eerily charged with its own impossibility. The whole project *of being* in a knowable world . . . is in the same way charged with its own impossibility. And yet, there the lovers are, two ultra-distinct faces on the screen, appearing in some definite sense on earth, among many such lovers, and in very real weather.

The soap-opera story was told from Scotty's point of view, the point of view of the one who could endure the loss and move indefinitely on; he looks into Dominique's impossible face, and into the vivid color and shape of various flowers, and she looks back at him. The sky itself blooms into particularity, as snow begins to fall. The lover moves through the strange clarity of specific places—sky, hospital, garden—and registers the startlingly specific things that compose these places—snow, flowers, their own faces—while he understands too well, and yet never well enough, that the maintenance of these clarities is temporary and bound to fail.

Poetic speech exists to look into the moment of this most difficult, most tentative, understanding of where we are, which is always both where and no where. It exists to look into the dark—though by no means with any assurances of a victory. I let the plot of the soap opera story remain essentially the same, but told it from the point of view of the beloved, the person faced with her very own impossibility. She is the one who faces death, and so, the one who is most inescapably real. And she is the one who needs, most deeply, to say good-bye—to Scotty, yes, but moreso to her own self. In the poem, the desire to postpone saying good-bye continues all around her; it might even be said to *mount* as she nears death. For her, to love an other comes to seem inadequate, small—it is overpowered by love of the ground itself, the ground the other was meant to stand for. She cannot help, from her position, but look intently into the dark, into whatever it is that becomes apparent as the ground itself begins to shatter. She comes to understand that what she has always been most toward is this—this dark. With this understanding in place, the motion of her lover's love has become a childish insistence on naming present specificities as though his naming them could make them eternal. His presence, then, for her, is the fearful postponing of what she now wants to want.

Pressed upon by Scotty's childish love, and by the obvious impossibility of owning the world, it occurred to me that Dominique need perform a kind of betrayal; she need give herself over to being possessed by the irreducible anonymity of the forces she is shaped, moved, and ultimately erased by. She does not so much stop loving . . . as turn love in a different direction, the direction of that darkness. Love not the scene, but the coming of a scene which can't be kept.

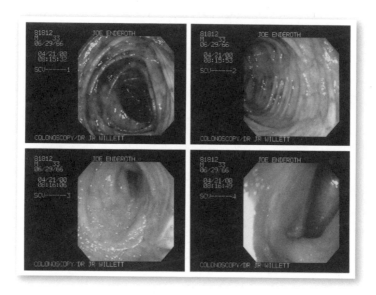

THE IMAGINARY TUNNEL

Martin Heidegger, in *What Is Called Thinking* (as translated by J. Glenn Gray), writes:

> What must be thought about, turns away from man. It withdraws from him. But how can we have the least knowledge of something that withdraws from the beginning, how can we even give it a name? Whatever withdraws refuses arrival. But—withdrawing is not nothing. Withdrawal is an event. In fact, what withdraws may even concern and claim man more essentially than anything present that strikes and touches him. Being struck by actuality is what we like to regard as constitutive of the actuality of the actual. However, in being struck by what is actual, man may be debarred precisely from what touches and concerns him—touches him in the surely mysterious way of escaping him by its withdrawal. The event of withdrawal could be what is most present in all our present, and so infinitely exceed the actuality of everything actual.

As a kid, *The Roadrunner* was never one of my favorite cartoons. It was too predictable, too pure in some sense—it never strayed from its strict essence. Indeed, it seemed that its whole intention was to make painfully obvious the eternal recurrence of its doomed action. And there was no speech; the logic of the image-narrative was never compromised, never overlaid with an other more distracted and/or distracting logic. Still, *The Roadrunner* never fell completely out of interest. There were even days when it seemed pleasing, almost as if I could feel a nostalgia for it before it had even moved into the past. Perhaps the very qualities that frustrated me were the same ones that, at the right hour, brought comfort. The vivid, deeply vacant space of the chase, with its one winding road and its reassuring repetition of a few landmarks (coupled with the repetition of a few choice sound effects) seemed soothing, and soothing in a way that no other cartoon could approach. It produced a kind of focus—not a focus that I possessed or could use, but a focus that paralyzed me. This focus allowed me to feel that my own imaginary space, like the bright desert of the chase, was bound up in some kind of joyful repetition—a joyfully eternal demonstration of pleasing figures.

A cartoon is a series of drawings, after all. It is a drawing into that which withdraws from the drawer—a drawing into that strange space that has learned to accommodate imagination. I believe that it is this strangely accommodating realm, taken as a whole and as the site of "what is," that Heidegger refers to when he says: "what must be thought about." Each drawing, on its own, begins as an attempt to create a picture of what has withdrawn from the drawer . . . but from the viewer's perspective, these attempts, considered separately, are never what the cartoon is. We don't see these drawings, one by one—we look instead into the realm that their being stitched together evokes; we look into and gather an action, which allows us to develop a sense of what withdraws from our every attempt to capture it.

And we are, to be sure, "claimed" by this event. It "concerns" us, for we understand implicitly that it is our only view on to "what must be thought about." That is, what claims us is not our failure to re-present, in any one picture, the real space we find ourselves faced with—what claims us is *the success* of the drawer, which is to say, the drawer's ability to withstand the failure of his every drawing, and to continue to locate, in some sense, an action. What we are, when we take care to watch a cartoon closely, is respect for the will of the drawer, re-spect—on-going indefinite spect— for that which is able to withstand the living nothingness that connects one scene, one drawing, to the next.

The Roadrunner strikes me as the most powerful of cartoons because it is able to demonstrate, keenly and unflinchingly, our relation to that which withdraws from us, that which "must be thought about." The coyote, clearly cast in the role of Heideggerian "man," is drawn into the roadrunner's withdrawal. Heidegger writes: "And what withdraws in such a manner keeps and develops its own incomparable nearness. Once we are so related to what withdraws, we are drawing into what withdraws, into the enigmatic and therefore mutable nearness of its appeal. Whenever man is properly drawing that way, he is thinking. . . ." This is surely the countenance of the coyote: the thinker. He is *possessed* by his consideration of how to better pursue what he most desires. It follows, then, that the roadrunner itself represents "what must be thought about." The roadrunner is more than the coyote's potential sustenance—it is the living symbol of his whole desire. The world wherein the coyote has successfully captured the roadrunner—the world in which the enigma is grasped and, presumably, devoured—is unthinkable to us. The moment the roadrunner is captured, *it ceases to be the roadrunner—* it ceases to be *that which withdraws*. The coyote, too, would cease to be "thinking," and so, cease to be the coyote. This unthinking, unmoving coyote, successfully alone with his desired object, is never the subject of the cartoon, and we might be grateful for that.

The coyote is "Wile E.," or wily—he is the thinker. What sort of thinking does he do? He thinks toward capturing the roadrunner. Many strategies exist for drawing nearer to an other, but the coyote is dominated by just one: technology. Implicit in the single-mindedness of this approach is the decision to give thinking altogether over to technology. This decision is not a decision that we see the coyote make—he seems instead to have been born into it, and there is never any indication that he could conceive of "thinking" in any other way. It is his "nature," we might say. Technology has claimed the coyote so decisively that he is no longer capable of doubting its promise; no matter how often it fails to capture what must be thought about, he cannot imagine another approach. Considering the remarkable persistence of his failure, we have to be struck by the stamina of his technologically scheming being. He re-appears after each failure with a strange confidence, even a vanity. He laughs to himself quietly, diabolically, as he assembles an ACME roadrunner-seeking robot. On his mail-box he has placed the word "genius" after his name. He has *never* captured—so far as we are given to know—what he most *needs* to capture, and yet he judges that his scheming abilities are supreme. The coyote seems to be defined by his inability to look into the past, where his string of humiliations lies quite unconcealed.

The Roadrunner offers really just this one character, the coyote, who represents man, the thinking animal. The roadrunner itself is not so much a character as a necessary image within the coyote's action. The narrative never unfolds from the roadrunner's point of view. The roadrunner *has* no point of view, no intentions, no life—its activity only makes sense within the coyote's actions. The roadrunner's personality is restricted to the essence of his eluding the coyote. The roadrunner is shrouded in the mystery of the elusive; it is utterly still or utterly moving, forever strangely erect and unspeakably entrenched in its never-kept-track-of way. It is silent, except for its signature honk—*meep meep*—which we hear at the beginning of the chase, initiating it, and then at the end of the chase, the signature of the eluding. This honk lets the coyote know that the roadrunner is there, that it is *near*. At the core of the roadrunner's honk there is a repeated *me* sound; thus, it is perhaps identity itself that the coyote comes near to, but cannot capture, or we could say conversely that it is at this point that the coyote *is himself*, for it is here that what must be thought about is beginning to elude him. We must look, though, to what precedes the moment of the eluding—we must look into the coyote's scheme—if we are to better understand the meaning of his failed nearness.

There is one episode, one failed scheme, that best illustrates the nature of the coyote's inability (technology's inability) to attain what he most desires, and it has to do with the point Heidegger raises about "the actuality of the actual." The episode I'm speaking of is the one wherein the coyote paints the image of a tunnel on to the side of the mountain. He then paints a road upon the ground to make it appear to lead into the imaginary tunnel. The roadrunner is meant, of course, to mistake the image of the tunnel for an actual tunnel, and so, to run into the mountain. This ploy is less conspicuously technological than most of the coyote's ploys—it involves no machinery, save a paintbrush—but it has arisen from the same knowledge, the same ability to manipulate natural conditions and thereby outsmart that nature. The ploy is also conspicuously successful—the roadrunner falls completely and without hesitation into the coyote's trap, running directly into the mountain. *But the mountain, for the roadrunner, is the tunnel.* That is, the roadrunner enters into the image as easily as it enters into the "actual." For the roadrunner, there seems to be no difference between the two. At this point, it becomes clear that the futility in which the coyote is immersed is more than circumstantial; *technology is, by its very nature, incapable of capturing what "man" means to capture.* Even when it succeeds, it fails.

The coyote does not immediately—or perhaps ever—understand this point, or if he does, he seems incapable of maintaining that understanding. When he sees the roadrunner enter into the tunnel, he assumes that the image has simply become "actual," and so he takes up chase. But *he* is not capable of entering into the image—he is somehow debarred from the realm of the image. In his effort to enter into the imaginary, he is "struck by the actuality of the actual," the mountain. If I recall correctly, there are two variations of this episode. In one, the coyote simply runs into the side of the mountain and falls back into his usual aching heap; in the other version, he is able, seemingly, to enter into the imaginary tunnel, whereupon he is immediately hit by an actual-and/or-imaginary train. The roadrunner, in this latter version, is conspicuous; he appears as the train's engineer, looking particularly happy, and he executes his gleeful honk as the train rushes over the coyote. His appearance leads us to suspect that there is a kind of cruelty at the heart of his withdrawal—that Someone Somewhere secretly cherishes the thinker's crushing mortality.

In both endings, though, the coyote's being debarred from the realm of the imaginary—his being subjected to the barely figure-able violence of the real—is very clear. It is equally clear that the roadrunner is quite at home in the imaginary, perhaps even inclined toward it. Thus, we can say that "what must be thought about" moves into the imaginary . . . and the thinker can follow only so far . . . until he is struck by the real, which is to say, by the unimaginary fact of his own body. Man, who prides himself in being both the masterful technician of the actual and the cunning manipulator of the imaginary, seeks above all something that, even as it endlessly penetrates and obsesses the "actual," cannot be reduced to it.

The roadrunner remains thoughtlessly aloft upon his way, his road, while the coyote, in pursuit, only ever finds the shock, the great crushing pain, of being on earth. For the coyote, the road is more than unsure—it is vengeful. Fortunately, the promise of technology is strong, and that promise maintains, mercifully, a kind of blindness for him, a mighty denial. Wile E. Coyote, blind in this way and endlessly entangled in the violence of his denial's strange machinery, is forever thrust into the mid-air . . . and is forever made to fall from a great height. It is fair to ask what we feel in this moment, witnessing this fall, this most definitive moment of his futility? Is it strange to say we feel a kind of pleasure?

For us, the moment of the roadrunner's decisive escape—which is at the same time the moment of the coyote's scheme's backfiring—produces *a return* that we find we have secretly wanted all along. The decisive withdrawal of the roadrunner is understood not only as a blow to the ego of the coyote; it is understood, more significantly, as a destruction of the whole way in which the thinking animal, the "genius," meant to capture and devour "what must be thought about." A great vanity, that is, is destroyed in the coyote's fall, and in this destruction we are allowed to see the coyote again—he comes out of concealment and re-inhabits his true condition: a body, alone, returned to the earth he should never have hoped to transcend in the first place.

Our desire to see this fall, and to feel the pain implicit in it, should not be thought of as sadistic. We understand that the coyote will persevere, no matter how much pain he brings down upon himself. His pain is never really the pain of losing something—it is the pain of gaining something—it is the pain of withstanding (standing-with) where he is. This is why we connect with him in that moment; we know that his pain restores him (even if only for this fleeting moment) to where he in truth belongs. We fully expect, of course, that he will crawl out from under the rock that crushed him and make his way back to his mailbox, where the next roadrunner-seeking ACME device is waiting. We do not lament this cycle—we cherish it as our own. We joy in the coyote's pain because that pain holds within it a variety of freedoms: above all, freedom from the machinery we ourselves have become entangled in, dulled for, and obscured by. As sacrilegious as it might sound, we are quite willing to condemn knowledge—that vain project—and the way that knowledge endlessly postpones our arrival at what cannot be possessed.

Often, in the climactic moment of the coyote's failure, there is a significant pause. He hangs in mid-air, having run off a cliff . . . and his eyes meet ours; we come together then—not in a knowledge that would empower us or secure us above nature, but in the knowledge of our being *subject* to nature. We come together with him in knowledge of the pain that must come, and this knowledge pleases us, if only because it unseats an imagination that meant to devour the mystery for which it moved. To look, at this moment, into Wile E. Coyote's eyes is uplifting, if only because it allows for an arrival *that is possible*—it allows for an arrival that restores us to the humility of our senses.

The coyote, representing "man," is in truth but a series of sketches, a series of posed figures arranged together so as to create an action. This figure, this action, is created by a series of drawings. Someone Somewhere sits at the drawing board, but then, when Someone Else sits and absorbs the action that his drawings create, that Someone Somewhere is absented. There's a strange familiar tension there—constant presence and constant absence in an intimate embrace. It is the tension of trying to see the Creator in the Creator's work. I feel like somehow *The Roadrunner* is emblematic of a new attitude toward this tension. Its action does not struggle to define "man," nor does it struggle to imply an awesome grandeur behind "man." Its Creator is instead implied as nothing more than a giddy witness to the violent disappointment of "man," which is to say, the continual undoing of his own creation. This Creator is not at home in what he creates—he is at home at the drawing board upon which he cannot be figured. Insofar as the action he constructs succeeds, he intersects with the viewer in the inevitable, un-despairing violence of the moment that undoes his every effort to know. Insofar as he succeeds, that is, we come to feel that the one true god is a trickster god; that the god who dumbfounds, foils, crushes, and annuls us . . . is on our side.

Acknowledgments

I thank very truly Matthew Zapruder for the help he provided as I edited this book. I thank Verse Press (especially Lori Shine!) for all of their work (past, present and future) having to do with the book. I thank J.J. for good work on the layout. I thank all of the journals that have published or will publish work from this book. I thank everyone who has afforded me a needed permission, especially Dr. Tim Boehme, whose permissions are as rare as they are delightful. I thank all the boys down at the lanes—bang bang, yabba dabba doo. I thank Tony, whose establishment, Tony's Place, I never cease to think of as my second home. Lastly I thank Ray Lou, whose terrible smallness, in the long run, clarifies what it is that we revere in others.

I thank Romana and Annika, my beloveds.

I should also say that I am very much in the debt of "Touch Me," a collection of poems and self-portrait photographs by avant-garde poet/self-portrait-photographer-artist, Suzanne Somers. Her daring and her vigorous self-love have obviously impacted upon me, and so, upon this book.

Joe Wenderoth grew up near Baltimore. He is Associate Professor of English at the University of California, Davis. Wesleyan University Press published his first two books of poems: *Disfortune* (1995) and *It Is If I Speak* (2000). Verse Press published *Letters to Wendy's* (2000). *Agony: A Proposal* is forthcoming.